THE ART OF
THE LEADER

William A. Cohen, Ph.D.

PRENTICE HALL
Englewood Cliffs, New Jersey 07632

Prentice-Hall International (UK) Limited, *London*
Prentice-Hall of Australia Pty. Limited, *Sydney*
Prentice-Hall Canada, Inc., *Toronto*
Prentice-Hall Hispanoamericana, S.A., *Mexico*
Prentice-Hall of India Private Limited, *New Delhi*
Prentice-Hall of Japan, Inc., *Tokyo*
Simon & Schuster Asia Pte. Ltd., *Singapore*
Editora Prentice-Hall do Brasil, Ltda., *Rio de Janeiro*

© 1990 *by*

William A. Cohen

10 9 8 7 6 5 4 3 2

Library of Congress Cataloging-in-Publication Data

Cohen, William A.,
   The art of the leader / by William A. Cohen.

   p. cm.
   ISBN 0-13-046657-3
   1. Leadership. I. Title
   HD57.7.C64 1990
   658.4'092—dc20   89-16359
                                                CIP

ISBN 0-13-046657-3

PRENTICE HALL
BUSINESS & PROFESSIONAL DIVISION
A division of Simon & Schuster
Englewood Cliffs, New Jersey 07632

PRINTED IN THE UNITED STATES OF AMERICA

MAY 1 7 1990

**This book is dedicated to the
United States Military Academy
that first showed me the way
and to the United States Corps of Cadets
who keep the spirit alive**

ACKNOWLEDGMENTS

To acknowledge the thousands who have contributed to this book over the years by their example, dedication, and self-sacrifice would not be possible. But I would like to acknowledge the following for special contributions:

Peter F. Drucker, Clarke Professor of Social Science, Claremont Graduate School

He annotated my first paper on leadership with the comment "Now I'm more confused than I was before." Since meeting him more than fourteen years ago he has helped me immeasurably by his example, criticism, and being Peter Drucker.

Major General Edward Barry, USAF

An outstanding leader in his own right, this old friend encouraged me by demanding my best in teaching leadership to senior officers of his command.

Captain Dana French, USN and Captain Dick Manning, USCG

They developed and taught an outstanding course in top level military leadership at the Industrial College of the Armed Forces, National Defense University. One of their students was the author.

COHEN'S MAXIMS

Compensation. Compensation, whether in the form of profit, salary, or job-satisfaction, is the by-product of your contribution to society and is in direct proportion to this contribution. It is an error to make compensation the focus of your life's work. You will not reach your full potential, and you will have cheated society of the full benefit of your talent and ability.

Duty. Whatever your occupation, you have a duty to the society of which you are a member. If you are a soldier, your duty is to protect that society. If you are in business or industry, your duty is to create and manage the jobs, wealth, and products of that society. Therefore, failure will be harmful not only to you, but also to society, just as success will be beneficial not only to you, but also to society.

Individual Ability. Every individual has the potential to do great things. To reach this potential it is necessary to discover your special abilities and qualifications. This means that you should always attempt new tasks and accept responsibility for untried assignments whenever they are offered.

Leadership. A leader accepts responsibility. This means that the welfare of those that you lead must always come before your own well-being. Therefore, while your primary duty is the accomplishment of your organization's mission, the welfare of your subordinates comes second, and your own welfare last.

Planning. Successful actions are not results of accidents or luck, but rather of an analysis of the situation and the preparation and proper execution of plans. Because of a changing environment and other variables, plans will not always succeed as originally conceived. But planning will maximize your successes and minimize your failures.

Responsibility. If you are assigned a task, you are responsible for its successful completion. There are no acceptable excuses for failing to fulfill this responsibility, and the responsibility cannot be shifted to others.

Risk. Never be afraid to take risks. If you work for someone, that is part of what you are getting paid for. If you work for yourself, it is the only way you can become successful.

Self-Confidence. Self-Confidence comes from successfully completing increasingly difficult tasks and assignments. Give your maximum to every project, no matter how insignificant or formidable.

Success. Success does not come from working hard. Success comes from playing hard. Therefore, if you want success, you must position yourself so that the duties that you perform, no matter how difficult or challenging, are considered play to you and not work. If you do this, not only will you gain success, but you will have fun doing it.

INTRODUCTION

I've been a student of leadership for more than forty years. From West Point to combat to the boardrooms of major corporations, I've seen leaders of all types operate in a wide variety of environments.

I thought I knew a lot about leadership, but one thing continued to puzzle me until fairly recently. There is a high demand for leaders everywhere. And leaders are well rewarded for what they do. Good leaders:

- Advance more quickly in organizations
- Receive more money and other material rewards
- Have greater prestige and more job security
- Have more control over their lives
- Get greater satisfaction from their jobs
- Are able to get groups that they lead to perform more productively

Of even greater concern, our country needs more good leaders of every type to lead countless thousands of companies, non-profit organizations, government departments, clubs, associations, schools, universities, churches, synagogues, and many other groups. If we don't get these leaders, our country will surely fail . . . maybe not in war . . . but just as importantly, in its ability to advance its society and the interests of its citizenry.

What was the one thing I couldn't figure out? With all of these incentives to becoming a leader, why aren't there more good leaders? This question stumped me.

Some say that leaders are born as leaders and come into existence in no other way. Thus their scarcity is as a result of Mother Nature. Research proves this wrong. Many leaders who later were acknowledged as great leaders went unrecognized for years.

I saw that many factors some thought important for leadership had little to do with being or becoming a good leader. These included education, wealth, years of experience, or even position in an organization.

Maybe you thought that you must be the formal manager of some organization to be a leader. I have seen hundreds of outstanding leaders who weren't formal managers of anything. Yet they and their organizations received significant benefits from their leadership.

If you are a manager or an executive, this fact is a compelling reason to become a leader now . . . and this book will help you to do so. But being a manager doesn't automatically make you a leader.

My inquiries finally yielded a very simple answer to my question as to why we don't have more good leaders. The answer was so obvious that I was surprised I overlooked it for so long. Maybe it was too obvious. The answer was this. A good many people that could become excellent leaders just didn't know how.

Just about anyone can become a competent leader. The only thing you need to know is what to do and then to do it.

As President Eisenhower told his son, "The one quality that can develop by studious reflections and practice is the leadership of men."[1]

Of course, Eisenhower was talking about his experiences during World War II. Once you know what to do, studious reflections and practice about leadership will help you in leading both sexes.

This may sound overly simplistic. The fact is that many intelligent, well-educated, motivated people that want to be good leaders simply don't know how to do it. And some of the things that they think they know about leadership are just plain wrong.

So what happens? They try. But without leadership know-how, its like a doctor doing brain surgery without being taught how. Maybe you can learn how eventually through experience. Chances are after your first big failure, you won't get the chance. Without knowledge of how to perform brain surgery, you are bound to make mistakes. Those mistakes will probably cause you to fail.

You can't perform brain surgery without knowing how to do it. And you can't lead successfully without knowing how to lead either.

Less than forty years ago, my professor and mentor, Peter Drucker said "Leadership is of utmost importance. Indeed there is no substitute for it."[2] But he went on to say that the first systematic book on leadership, written by Xenophon three thousand years ago was still the best book on the subject. Still it failed to enable people to learn how to become leaders . . . and so did books, papers, and speeches written after Xenophon.

I believe that Drucker meant this in the sense that one must start

---

[1]Stephen E. Ambrose, *Eisenhower: Vol. 1* (Simon and Schuster: New York, 1983).
[2]Peter F. Drucker, *The Practice of Management* (Harper and Row: New York, 1955) p. 194

with some basic capacity for leadership. Yet this capacity may lie invisible and dormant. Because one does not start life as a general, company president, or outstanding leader.

As General William Tecumseh Sherman, famous, or infamous depending on your point of view, for his "march to the sea" during the Civil War expressed it: "I have read of men born peculiarly endowed by nature to be a general . . . but I have never seen one."

General Maxwell D. Taylor, former paratrooper general during World War II and later Chief of Staff of the Army felt the same way. In a lecture on leadership to the Industrial College of the Armed Forces in the Spring of 1977 he said, ". . . there seems no reason to doubt that the leadership qualities . . . are susceptible to being taught and learned."[3]

That's why I wrote this book. There are no "blue sky" theories to master. The emphasis of the book is on how to do it. The leadership techniques that I will show you have proved effective over thousands of years. They will work for you as they did for Julius Caesar, Abraham Lincoln, or George S. Patton.

I have used a lot of examples to illustrate every technique. I have especially used military examples. More than that, I have consciously attempted to apply leadership techniques learned "the hard way" in battle to everyday leadership problems you will run into in the company and elsewhere. I have done this because leadership in battle represents a worst case scenario. There are few leadership situations as severe or as challenging or with more risk and uncertainty. If you know how to lead others on the battlefield, you can lead others in the office, on the salesforce, in the boy or girl scout troop, in the church or synagogue, or anywhere else.

In preparation for writing this book, I went back and relearned everything I thought I knew about leadership. I also investigated almost every new concept and read almost every book. I interviewed many general officers for their ideas. Some of these generals had been my students in my leadership seminars.

In the fall of 1988, I was on active duty as a reserve officer in the Air Force. I was extremely fortunate in being able to attend a top level leadership course taught at National Defense University in Washington, D.C. Several four star generals and admirals helped to

---

[3]Maxwell D. Taylor, "Military Leadership: What Is It? Can It Be Taught?" *Distinguished Lecture Series* (National Defense University: Washington, D.C.)

teach this incredible course. Here I could see leadership from the perspective of a Chairman of the Joint Chiefs of Staff, a Chief of Naval Operations, or a Commander-in-Chief of an entire geographical area. It added immeasurably to the breadth of my own perspective.

I know that what you will learn from this book works. I can't guarantee that you will become a general, admiral, or company president. But if you act on what you will learn in it, you will become more competent as a leader. And no one can say that you can't become whatever you want.

From this book and these techniques you will learn:

- How to Take Charge in Any Situation
- How to Win a Group's Loyalty and Respect
- How to Build Your Organization Like a Winning Football Team
- How to Double or Triple Your Organization's Productivity
- How to Lead Others AT Your Level
- How to Lead Your Boss
- When It Is Important *Not* to Lead
- Seven Ways to Get Anyone to Follow You
- How to Use the Seven Influence Strategies
- How to Develop Confidence as a Leader Yourself

This introduction is too long already. Turn to Chapter 1 and let's get started in becoming a top notch leader today!

CONTENTS

Chapter 1

THE POWER OF LEADERSHIP

Leadership has an extraordinary power. It can make the difference between success and failure in anything you do for yourself or any group you belong to. I know this is a strong statement, but in this chapter I will give you examples to prove what I say. Further, I will show you that becoming a first-class leader is a lot easier than you may have thought.

How One Man Made the Difference

As a young Air Force lieutenant I was a member of the 11th Bomb Wing at Altus Air Force Base in Oklahoma. This unit had been one of the finest B-52 bombing wings in Strategic Air Command, and had been the only wing to win the coveted Fairchild Trophy three times for competition in bombing accuracy. This unit was also one of the few wings never to have failed an organizational readiness inspection. Aircrews were consistently superior in navigation, bombing, aerial refueling, and other flying techniques.

Unfortunately, over a period of months, the unit had begun to drift. We failed to do some of our training requirements successfully. We made some late takeoffs because of maintenance problems. Our sense of mission disappeared. We failed an important test of our flying and combat skills. Once we had ranked as one of the top three combat wings based on a point system maintained on a weekly basis. On the same system, we were now ranked dead last.

On alert with my crew one evening, I received a hurried call from base operations. "There's a new commander on base. His name is Colonel Kyes. Stay out of his way."

We couldn't stay out of his way because Colonel Kyes visited us that night. He cancelled all leaves of absence. All "free time" of any sort was rescinded until further notice. This included weekends and even crew rest after flight. Colonel Kyes moved commanders and staff he judged to be lacking to less responsible positions on the spot. He encouraged others to retire. No career or individual was sacred.

Colonel Kyes met with each of the 1500 officers and airmen reporting to him. He told us where we were going . . . back to number one—and how we were going to get there. He said we would brief him personally on every mission flown before we could fly it. Pilots had to know as much about the target as their bombardiers and navigators, who in turn had to be able to back up their pilots.

If you wanted a transfer, Colonel Kyes would get you one. If you stayed in the wing, you were going to work your fanny off. And this was in peacetime!

At first, we hated Kyes. Our wives and girlfriends hated Kyes. Those whose careers he hurt especially hated him, and some left the Air Force.

Then our hard work began to show results. Our bombs hit on target. We took off exactly at take-off time, and our aircraft systems worked as they had never worked before. We had a surprise readiness inspection, and not only passed, but scored higher than we ever had in the past. We were ranked number one.

A strange thing began to happen. We felt pride in ourselves and pride in Colonel Kyes as our commander. Our hate turned to respect. When Colonel Kyes left the 11th Bomb Wing on his promotion to Brigadier General, there was a genuine sense of loss. Our respect had by then turned to love.

Colonel Kyes eventually wore the three stars of a lieutenant general; but for an untimely death, I believe he would have attained the fourth star of a full general.

General Kyes's life taught me some important lessons about leadership and the difference one individual can make in helping an organization to reach its goals. And I have seen that lesson repeated again and again. I have seen it in organizations large and small, formal and informal, military and civilian. The lesson is that one individual and his or her leadership make all the difference between success and failure.

The Amazing Fact as to Why Some of the World's Best Known Men and Women Succeeded

Leadership has to do with getting things accomplished by acting through others. Regardless of your own abilities, there are many important goals that you cannot attain without the help of others.

Around the turn of the century, a young newsman by the name of Napoleon Hill interviewed steel magnate Andrew Carnegie. Andrew Carnegie was then one of the wealthiest men alive. He convinced Hill to devote twenty years of his life to a study of what made men successful. Carnegie helped Hill by giving him introductions to the mightiest, wealthiest, and best-known men of his day. These included Henry Ford, Theodore Roosevelt, Charles Schwaub, George Eastman, John D. Rockefeller, Thomas Edison, Julius Rosenwald, Clarence Darrow, and many others.

Napoleon Hill discovered an amazing fact from his research. No successful individual became successful strictly by himself or by virtue of what he could do by himself. Every single one of the successful individuals that Napoleon Hill had interviewed had become successful through the help of others. These other individuals had a greater talent in some area.

Who were these others? They were bosses, colleagues, and subordinates. Without them, not a single person interviewed by Hill would have become successful.

Carnegie himself must have recognized this, because on his tombstone he had engraved a single sentence. "Here lies one who knew how to get around him men who were cleverer than himself."

While an MBA student at the University of Chicago, I found support for Hill's conclusion. A study of hundreds of top executives showed that every single one, whether in business, government, or the military, had a sponsor. What is a sponsor? A sponsor is someone who has actually promoted an executive's success at one or more points in his or her career. No one has made it to the top of any organization without a sponsor.

What does this mean? Quite clearly it means that you can reach the most difficult and important goals only with the help of others. Like Colonel Kyes, you can be successful only through exercising good leadership and helping others to reach their goals.

Why You Don't Need to Be a Manager to Be a Leader

Once I met a young engineer at a major aerospace company. He had become director of a major program although he was barely thirty. I was very much interested in how this came about. Here's the story as a vice-president told it to me.

Once a year there was a savings bond drive in this company. No one wanted the job of getting employees to sign up for additional bond deductions from their paychecks. Since no one wanted the job, they assigned this duty to the most junior engineer. Most did the minimum work possible and made no serious attempt at convincing people to make additional investments.

Somebody must have forgotten to tell this youngster, because he really took charge. He convinced every engineer and manager present in his department to buy, and he didn't stop there. He called all over the country to talk to engineers who were at temporary duty elsewhere. He got them all charged up. "Look," he would say, "at the end of this bond drive, they post results, and our organization is competing with others. We can be number one."

Amused, at first the old timers bought bonds for this reason. Then almost in spite of themselves they became excited. They became excited solely because of this new engineer. No one had ever appealed to them in this way before. Of course this organization finished in first place by a country mile, but that wasn't the end of it. The department head noticed that although savings bonds had very little to do with engineering, the bond drive had helped to increase productivity. People just seemed to feel better about themselves as a member of the organization and wanted to perform better. When they actually won, they really felt good!

The president of the company noticed the unusual bond drive results and asked about them. He remembered this young engineer's name, and knew that if this engineer could accomplish so much with a bond drive, he would accomplish even more as a manager.

Only four months later when an opening occurred, this young man was promoted over twenty other engineers who had more seniority in the company. It shouldn't surprise you that it wasn't too long after I met him that they promoted this young man again. You guessed it. This time they made him a vice-president, and you just know that he will be president some day.

Note that this engineer was a strong leader before he held an official position in the organization as a manager. I'll have more to say about this throughout the book.

How You Can Lead *Before* You Are Promoted

You may have heard someone say, "I'll wait till I'm promoted. Then I'll have an opportunity to demonstrate my leadership." That's like the old story about the freezing man and the wood-burning stove. The man looked at the wood-burning stove and spoke these words. "Give me heat and then I will give you wood."

You may laugh because everyone knows that you have to put wood on a fire before a fire will give you heat. The same is true about promotion. If you want to get promoted, you have to be a leader first. Then someone will promote you.

Tom Peters, the coauthor of *In Search for Excellence, A Passion for Excellence*, and other books, found similar situations in organizations he studied. All excellent companies had strong leaders at every level. Some were managers and some were not. I want to repeat this. Some were managers and some were not, but all were strong leaders. Therefore, you don't need to wait to be promoted to be a leader.

You don't even have to be in an organization to be a strong leader. You can start your own organization. Jimmy Calano and Jeff Salzman, started a company called Career Tracks Seminars almost right out of college. Within a few years, these two men found themselves at the head of one of the largest seminar companies in the country. They accomplished this by offering a quality product at a lower price than their competition.

Do Calano and Salzman give these seminars themselves? Absolutely not! Those who give the seminars are individuals who have had years and years of experience, many with advanced degrees in their particular fields. Jimmy Calano and Jeff Salzman don't have to be the experts. They are the leaders. Through their leadership, their employees have made them successful.

Good leaders attract others who are happy to help them achieve success. It is easier than you think to become a good leader. You can become a good or superior leader with others wanting to follow and to help you. They will help you achieve your goals because you will help them to achieve theirs.

The Leadership Model That Will Help You to Lead

I would like to propose a model of leadership. A model is only a theoretical representation of something real. It can have considerable value if the representation is accurate. Why? Because we can apply the model to a wide variety of situations without having to develop a new representation each time. Having found what works once, we can then apply the theory effectively again and again.

Now let's talk first about the model of leadership that I would like to propose I want to propose to you what I call the combat model of leadership. Why do I recommend combat as a model? The most difficult circumstances in which a leader must lead are in combat. There is a great risk. There is considerable uncertainty due to confusion, changing circumstances, and lack of information. There may be considerable hardship because of the environment or actions of the enemy. There is a significant penalty for failure or reward for success.

Combat is probably the most severe environment in which you will ever lead other human beings in accomplishing any goal. If you can apply the combat model of leadership successfully, you can be successful in leading in many other difficult, but less demanding, environments.

General John T. Chain, Jr., Commander-in-Chief of the Strategic Air Command, said recently, "Military decisions are made in the fog of war, resulting in a significant degree of uncertainty about the validity of the very information on which the most critical decisions are made. Decisions must be made quickly and with life-and-death results. Coupled simultaneously with the need to deal with this uncertainty is the military leader's task of inspiring confidence in subordinate commanders and cohesiveness in the troops."[1]

General Frederick J. Kroesen knows something about combat leadership. He fought in World War II, Korea, and Vietnam. During this time, he rose from second lieutenant to four-star general as Commander-in-Chief, U.S. Army, Europe, and the Central Army Group of NATO. Since leaving the Army, he has worked with corporations and other organizations on a variety of management and defense issues. During a meeting at which I was present, a friend asked General Kroesen about differences between leadership in the military and corporations. Said General Kroesen. "The principles of leadership aren't different. Where you have a successful leader, you have a successful corporation."[2]

What is the combat model? Well, another man who might know something about the combat model of leadership was General George S. Patton. Again and again, General Patton proved his abilities to lead men in combat. He led small groups during in his career as well as large numbers of men—hundreds of thousands. And he frequently did this while overcoming incredible obstacles under severe hardship and risk of death.

During World War I, Patton was a 29-year-old colonel commanding the first American tanks in combat. The first use of the tank was to protect against machinegun fire and artillery while crossing difficult terrain. The tank had one big problem. It was difficult to see out of. So Patton led his tanks by accompanying them on foot!

He was once wounded while doing this. Notning is without a price, and that was a price he was willing to pay. Patton's leadership brought victory on the battlefield as well as personal fame and fortune.

Patton defined leadership as the art of getting your subordinates to do the impossible. Is such a definition also applicable to civilian pursuits? Let's see.

Some years ago there was a small aerospace company located in the foothills of southern California. This small company of 350 employees made oxygen masks and other life-support equipment for military and civilian flyers.

The firm's main competitor was another small company located on the east coast. Both companies competed heavily for government contracts in a number of areas.

During a particularly bitter competition involving pilot crash helmets, the West Coast company ran into extreme difficulty. Part of the reason was the higher salaries on the west coast. Also, all hourly employees received "time and a half" for overtime. But the biggest problem was that everyone had a "business as usual" attitude. From worker to manager, they did their jobs. If the company was in trouble, that was someone else's problem. They were doing the best that they possibly could. Or so they thought.

Then the company suddenly ran out of cash. With no cash reserves, it could not produce its goods. It could not meet payrolls. It had other problems. Seeing no way out, the president of the company committed suicide. The company went into "Chapter 11." Under this chapter of the bankruptcy law, the bank tries to save the company through its own control.

In desperation, the bank sought someone experienced who could lead the company out of its troubles. Where was the unusual person who was willing to work at minimum salary? Where was someone who had the supreme self-confidence that he would be successful under these conditions? After a difficult search they found a young man by the name of Aaron Bloom. Aaron Bloom had been a vice-president of engineering who had left the same firm several years earlier.

Bloom took charge of the company. Gathering the less than 50 employees that remained together, he made an announcement. "From eight in the morning until five in the afternoon, we will all perform our regular duties. If you are a secretary, you'll do secretarial work. If you're a manager, you'll manage. If you are a design engineer, you'll design. After five o'clock, everyone, from secretaries to myself, will help the production line put the product together. You and I will take our orders from the production supervisors. There will be no pay for this, but there will be sandwiches for supper."

Bloom answered questions and then concluded: "We are going to return this company to its rightful place of saving lives by supplying a quality product at a good price. We are also going to save our jobs. I know we can do this. If I thought we couldn't, I wouldn't be here."

Within two years, this small aerospace firm had returned to its former position and even more so. Once again, it was vibrant with a full complement of employees necessary to fulfill its mission. Once again, the company was profitable. Clearly the company was on top due solely to the leadership of one man, Aaron Bloom.

One interesting thing to me was that everyone worked hard to turn the company around. And remember, they did so without extra compensation.

An even more interesting question is why they didn't do this before they went into Chapter 11? Had they done so, they would not have run out of money. No one would have been fired. No one would have had to work this hard. Why didn't they do this? Why was it necessary that 300 members of the company had to leave its employ before this happened? And how could it be that 50 people could do more than 350 had done?

I have thought a great deal about this question and I'll tell you my answer. I don't believe that the 350 employees knew they could make a difference. Further, I don't believe they cared. Aaron Bloom made them see that they could do it and made them care. He had them do the impossible.

Leadership Is Getting People to Perform
to Their Maximum Potential

Let me propose a definition of leadership to you. With this definition, it doesn't make any difference whether you are leading a company, an organization, a military unit, or just some friends in a club. Leadership is the art of influencing others to their maximum performance to accomplish any task, objective, or project.

Note that my definition of leadership says nothing about management. We saw earlier that leadership and management are not the same.

Can you always get people to perform to their maximum potential? I believe that through leadership you can. Consider this for a moment. Have you ever done something that was very difficult? You thought you had finished, and than found that you had to do it all over again. It's frustrating, and it's hard to perform the second time to our maximum.

Once I spent six hours doing an audio taping with a publisher before we found that the taping had gone all wrong, and had to be done again from the beginning. It was very difficult to repeat what we had considered our original maximum performance.

Once you know that something is completed, you feel you've done all you can. There's a tremendous psychological letdown, and it's very difficult to build up to that psychological peak again. If it's hard to get ourselves to do something again, you know it's difficult to get people we lead to do it.

Do you remember seeing the television series "Baa Baa Black Sheep" several years ago? That series was the story of Colonel Pappy Boyington, a unique marine commander during World War II. Boyington led his fighter squadron, the Black Sheep, against the Japanese. Under Boyington's leadership, the Black Sheep became the highest scoring squadron in the Pacific in enemy planes shot down. Yet the Black Sheep were all rejects from other combat squadrons, thus their name.

At one point, the Black Sheep had been in combat for a fairly long time. They received word that the following day they would withdraw from combat for rest and relaxation some miles behind the lines.

What do you think happens in a combat squadron when its members know that their last combat mission is over for a while? Having been in such a squadron myself, I can tell you that the squadron makes one gigantic party. And the consumption of alcoholic beverages goes up significantly. This is exactly what the Black Sheep did.

After several hours, most were either sleeping or in a semi-conscious haze, awaiting their coming departure.

Colonel Boyington himself was about ready to turn in when suddenly a radio call came in. The worried radio operator ran up to the colonel and gave him a weary salute. "Colonel Boyington," he said, "I hate to tell you this, but look at this message." Pappy Boyington read the message. It read as follows:

Before being withdrawn from combat, essential that you bomb targets in Rabaul tonight.

Pappy Boyington couldn't believe his eyes. He didn't know what to do. His entire squadron had just had the biggest party of their lives. They were now no longer disposed to walk, much less fly on a combat mission. How could he get them to do exactly that? How could any leader get his subordinates to do anything under these circumstances?

Pappy Boyington strolled to the center of the quonset hut where the Black Sheep were sleeping and turned on the lights. He put his hands on his hips, looked around and shouted loud enough for the entire barracks to hear. "Are any of you guys drunk enough to come with me and bomb Rabaul tonight? Because that's what I'm doing and I'm taking off in fifteen minutes."

One of the Black Sheep looked up, blinked his eyes, and said, "I'll go with you, Pappy." Several others mumbled something about "that sounds like fun."

Before you knew it, Pappy Boyington had his flight of Black Sheep. They went out together, and they bombed Rabaul. They did combat again, even though a few hours earlier they had thought that their combat was over.

To Lead, You Must First Win Minds

Now, I don't know what this says to you. What it says to me is this: A good deal of leadership has to do with your ability to win the minds of the people around you. If you can do this, you'll not only lead successfully, but you'll be successful in achieving your goals and objectives.

What we've seen is that the power of leadership is considerable. The resources of your organization, top management actions, actions of adversaries, the abilities of people who you're responsible for or who are in your organization, or anything else, are all secondary. They are secondary to your ability to help people do things that they didn't know they could do or didn't know needed to be done. To do this, you must first win their minds to your way of thinking.

Proof That Leaders Are Made, Not Born

You may have heard that great leaders are born with the characteristics necessary to make them leaders. All of us are either born with these characteristics or not. If you don't have these characteristics at birth, you're out of luck. There is nothing you can do about it.

The preceding theory is absolute nonsense. It is true that people are born with certain characteristics that give them the potential for excelling at certain things. Some people are born with a talent for playing basketball, being a great concert pianist, or being a leader. However, learning and developing whatever abilities you have is far more important than the abilities that you were born with.

Want proof? Researchers have found that you have a better chance of becoming a company president if you are more than six feet tall than if you are less than six feet. This would seem to support the "born with" theory. Doesn't being tall say something of your chances of becoming a top leader?

The only problem is that there are just too many exceptions. Napoleon Bonaparte was short. So were Gandhi, Truman, and Ulysses S. Grant. Colonel Kyes, who led his wing so successfully that he became a three-star general, was five feet seven inches tall. David Ben Gurion, the first Prime Minister of the modern state of Israel, was only five foot three inches. His famous general, Moshe Dayan, was five foot eight inches. The first man in my West Point class to make general was five feet ten inches. There are tens of thousands of company presidents who are less than six feet tall. If you are wondering about my height, I'm four inches short of six feet.

The Famous Air Force General Who Was Once Considered a Poor Leader

Let me tell you about someone who was taller than six feet, and who definitely learned to be a great leader. And I know that he *learned* leadership because one of those who taught him told me about it.

Hoyt S. Vandenberg became a four-star general and Chief-of-Staff of the U.S. Air Force. He was a unique leader. During World War II when he commanded the 9th Air Force, he frequently visited his squadrons at their bases. On one occasion a gunner from one of the crews had a complete breakdown. "I can't go today," the gunner screamed. "I won't fly today, sir. I can't go today!" he protested to his aircraft commander.

General Vandenberg saw the disturbance. Running up to the gunner he placed his hand on his shoulder. "Sergeant, you don't have to go today. This is not your day. This one is mine." With that, General Vandenberg climbed into the airplane and flew the mission as a gunner. You can imagine its effects on the 9th Air Force. It also must have had a positive effect on the gunner, as he stayed and flew the additional missions necessary to complete his tour of duty.

General Vandenberg was not a born leader. How do I know? When I was a Cadet at West Point, one of my best friends was my classmate Ted Wells. Ted's father and his grandfather had also graduated from the academy. Shortly before our graduation, I was sitting with Ted and talking to his grandfather, Major General Robert M. Danford. General Danford had graduated in the class of 1904, and had long since retired from the army.

"Bill," he said, "I understand that you're going into the Air Force."

"Yes, sir," I said, "I am. I want to fly."

"Well," he said, "you know I was Commandant of Cadets under General MacArthur when he was a Superintendent of the Military Academy after World War I. Have you heard of General Hoyt Vandenberg?"

"Oh, yes sir," I said. "He was Chief-of-Staff of the Air Force ten years ago."

"I'll tell you something I bet you didn't know about General Vandenberg. When I was Commandant, General Vandenberg was a plebe going through his first year at the Academy. General Vandenberg was at one point almost discharged from the Academy."

"Why?" I asked.

General Danford smiled. "Because of a lack of leadership ability," he answered.

General Vandenberg developed himself from the time he was a plebe at West Point to the time that he graduated. He became a great leader not because he was born a leader, but because he learned how to lead and developed into one.

Why Good Leadership Doesn't Depend on Good Deals

I've mentioned this before, but I want to mention it again: Good leadership doesn't seem to have much to do with participation in management or Japanese management or good working conditions or superior pay. You don't have to be a "nice guy."

In western Pennsylvania, there's a tool and die company called Oberg Industries. The president is Don Oberg. A magazine article in *INC* magazine called him "The Lord of Discipline."

Western Pennsylvania is right in the middle of union country, but Oberg Industries is nonunionized. It's not because of pleasant working conditions. Oberg Industries has a fifty-hour work week with a fifteen-minute lunch break for both management and labor.

Here are some other interesting facts. In a recent year, annual sales for most tool-and-die companies were on the average $2 million a year. At Oberg they were $27 million. And the average sales per employee was 30 percent higher. There was no recession the year that we're talking about. It may be hard to believe, but 1,600 people applied for only thirty job openings that year.

Now, why is this? Are Oberg employees well paid? Of course they are. However, far more important than compensation, Don Oberg, while he is a hard task master, has managed to instill in all his employees the idea that if you work at Oberg, you're the best. Furthermore, everyone knows that the leader at the top is giving 100 percent himself to be the best. And so Oberg continues to outperform similar firms and people fight to work there.[3]

Good leadership doesn't depend on good deals. Let's look again at our combat model of leadership. You've probably heard that many of our outstanding combat organizations are elite units: Green Berets, Rangers, Marines, the Navy's SEALS, airborne units, fighter squadrons, and others.

Members of these units often receive additional compensation. The official name is hazardous duty pay. If you think that hazardous duty pay amounts to quite a bundle, you're dead wrong. Not only is it not a lot, but it certainly doesn't make up for the additional risks that individuals in these organizations face.

Furthermore, in some of these organizations, promotions are slower than in comparable regular military units. And they frequently train much longer hours. Why, then, do people volunteer for elite units?

How I Learned What It Means to Be an Air Commando

In the Southeast Asian conflict, I was an air commando. I flew as a member of the 609th Air Commando Squadron, flying in A-26s at night, and attacking truck convoys in a heavilly defended, mountainous area.

Flying low on a night interdiction mission, these mountainous formations called "Karst" caused many tragedies. The enemy used every weapon they could get their hands on from small caliber ZPU machine guns, to 37 mm, 57 mm, and 85 mm anti-aircraft artillery.

Yet in the Air Commandos we flew an old World War II aircraft which the old Army Air Force used for the first time in 1944. This was 1968! The 609th Air Commando Squadron won the Presidential Unit Citation for its gallantry in combat. The price was the highest per sortie aircraft loss rate in the Vietnam War.

What made us do this? On our flying suit we wore a special insignia patch that proclaimed us a "Nimrod." This was also our radio call sign. Nimrod, in the Bible, was the first hunter. This patch said that its wearer had over 100 missions in the aircraft: all night strikes. We wore it proudly.

When I returned to the states, my assignment was to Wright-Patterson Air Force Base, at Dayton, Ohio. I had a nonflying job as a program manager in charge of development of aircraft life support equipment. Once a month I would put on my flying suit and fly to maintain flying skill.

A few months after I returned, I was walking along in my flying suit on my way to the flight line. A car suddenly stopped directly opposite me across the street. The driver, another officer with his wife next to him, called out, "Could you come over a minute, Captain?"

I went over to the car, and the officer introduced himself. He had flown another type of aircraft in another squadron from my base. However, he wasn't thinking about himself or what he had done. Instead he turned to his wife and pointed to my "Nimrod" patch with respect. "Honey, this is one of the fellows I was telling you about. This is an air commando. He's a Nimrod." Once again, leadership does not depend on good deals or pleasant working conditions or compensation. People will readily follow you in very difficult circumstances for other reasons . . . if you know how to lead.

Seven Facts You Must Know Before You Begin to Lead

1. One person can make the difference between success or failure in any organization. You can be that person through becoming a leader.

2. One of the most amazing facts is that most people become successful only through the help of others. You can obtain this help through the practice of leadership.

3. You don't need to be a manager to be a leader. You don't need to wait to be promoted. You can become a leader immediately.

4. If you learn the basic elements of the combat model of leadership, you will be able to lead in just about any other situation. This is because combat presents the most severe leadership challenge in risk, uncertainty, environmental hardship, and the penalty for failure or reward for success.

5. The essence of leadership is very simple. It is to motivate people to perform to their maximum potential to achieve goals or objectives that you set.

6. Leaders are made, not born. If you want to be a leader, you can learn how in the same way that you learned other skills.

7. Good leadership doesn't depend on good deals or pleasant working conditions. Your ability to motivate people to perform to their maximum is independent of these factors.

Leadership has tremendous power to help you to accomplish anything that you want the group or organization that you lead to achieve. You can tap this power through learning to apply relatively simple techniques. Let's start right out in Chapter 2, "Six Ways to Get the Combat Model to Work for You."

ENDNOTES

[1]"CINCSAC's Views on Professional Military Education," *Air Force Policy Letter for Commanders* (October 1988), p. 2.

2 This comment was made at a presentation to a group of students of the Industrial College of the Armed Forces at Ft. McNair, Washington, DC, on October 4, 1988.

3 Donna Fenn, "The Lord of Discipline," *INC* (November, 1985), pp. 82–85, 88, 90, 95.

Chapter 2

SIX WAYS TO GET THE COMBAT MODEL TO WORK FOR YOU

How can you or anyone else carry out the combat model of leadership? Here are six ways to make the combat model work for you:

1. Be Willing to Take Risks
2. Be Innovative
3. Take Charge
4. Have High Expectations
5. Maintain a Positive Attitude
6. Get Out in Front

Let's look at each of these in turn.

Be Willing to Take Risks

You may have heard of the adage "No guts, no glory." It's like the body builder's adage, "No pain, no gain." Ask yourself, what is the worst that can happen? Accept that, and then press on.

A small company had tried for years to get in the business of building gas masks for the U.S. Army. A large multimillion dollar company that was fifty times the size of the smaller company had all of that business. The large company had hundreds of engineers. The smaller company had only five. The large company had done almost all the work on gas masks for the Army for the previous thirty-five years. The smaller company had never even had a single gas mask contract before. The only difference was in the leadership of the two organizations.

The responsible manager in the smaller company absolutely believed that he and his engineers could do the impossible. He was willing to risk his reputation, company resources, and other opportunities to bid a $2 million gas mask contract. The largest new product development contract ever bid previously was $200,000. He convinced his boss, the company president, that he could do this. More importantly, he convinced his five engineers.

They worked and researched, and did everything they could think of. They made many trips across country to visit their potential customer. They read everything they could find out about the use of gas masks and their development. For thirty days they labored, putting together the best bid proposal that they possibly could. Then they sent in their proposal and bid the contract.

After all of this work you probably think that the smaller company deserved to win. Maybe, but they did not. Neither did the rival company. Because of budgetary problems, the government agency made the decision to delay procurement for a year. Both companies were to have the chance to re-study the problem and propose anew.

What this did was to raise the ante. Now both companies had to invest additional time and resources into the project. Still only one would win, and the odds were still with the larger company. The research and development leader in the smaller company decided to risk again. He asked his engineers to redouble their efforts, and if there was any doubt before, now these engineers really believed they could win.

A year later they bid the contract again and they won. That single contract led the company into a business worth millions of dollars in sales a year. The reason was one individual's leadership and his willingness to risk. No guts, no glory.

Be Innovative

During World War I, General Douglas MacArthur was a 38-year-old brigadier general, and brand new brigade commander in France. He went forward and waited in the trenches with the battalion that was going to lead the way in a major attack.

He called the battalion commander. "Major," he said, "when the signal comes to go over the top, I want you to go first, before your men.

He paused and then continued, "If you do this, your battalion will follow you. You will earn the Distinguished Service Cross and I will see that you get it."

He looked the Major over for several long moments. "I see you are going to do it. You have it now."

So saying, MacArthur unpinned a Distinguished Service Cross from his own uniform and pinned it on the uniform of the Major.

Now, I ask you, what happened when that signal came to go over the top? Well, you know as well as I do. The Major, proudly wearing a Distinguished Service Cross which he had not yet actually earned, charged out in front of his troops. And as MacArthur had forecast, his troops followed behind him. As a result, they were successful in securing their objective.[1]

Take Charge

If you want to lead, you've got to take charge.

During the Civil War, Ulysses S. Grant planned the first combined land/sea operation at the Battle of Fort Donelson. Before he could implement this operation, the senior Union Army commander ordered him to a conference. While he was away, the operation began.

As almost always happens, the operation did not go as planned. There were a number of mishaps. The Union sea attack was repulsed. The Confederates attacked Grant's right wing, and it was collapsing. As his right wing was disintegrating, Grant arrived on the battlefield.

He stopped to blame no one. What he did was to draw his saber and, galloping back and forward on horseback along the front line, shouted to his men. "Fill your cartridge cases quick; the enemy is trying to escape and must not be permitted to do so.

And they did. Through Grant's actions, the Union troops rallied and won the battle.[2]

Have High Expectations

Research has shown that the higher the goals you have, the higher the goals you will achieve.

As a professor, I have my students participate in an exercise in pricing. One group gets this confidential information:

"Your company designs computer systems for business. Yesterday you received an emergency notice from top management. This message told you that you must withdraw and junk one of your older models, the XC-1000 computer, immediately. This is due to the implementation of a government regulation requiring additional features to prevent tampering which this model does not have.

"Unfortunately, you cannot modify the XC-1000, as it was built to last forever. You can't even use it for parts. By law, you must sell or get rid of all computer systems such as the XC-1000 by the third of April. (This is the second of April.) If not, you cannot offer it to the market at any price, or even give it away.

"Fortunately, you have only one of the XC-1000s left in inventory. In fact, you haven't sold an XC-1000 in over three years. This morning your assistant contacted the Acme Junk Company. They will pick up your XC-1000 and melt it down so they can sell it for scrap, at no charge to you.

"Before you can make final arrangements, you receive a call from Consolidated Unlimited. Their director of MIS would like to meet with you tomorrow about the possible immediate purchase of a XC-1000. You told him there was one left, and that the price was negotiable. You delay your arrangements with Acme and begin preparing for your meeting.

"Do not reveal any of this information to any person not on your team. Complete the answers to the following questions. You will have thirty minutes.

1 For what price do you expect to sell the XC-1000, and why?

2. What is the lowest price you would accept, and why?

3. What is your strategy for your meeting tomorrow?"

I designate another group as buyers. They also receive confidential information. Their information reads as follows:

"Several years ago you became Director of MIS of Consolidated Unlimited, a small company manufacturing copper tubing. One of your first actions was to buy an XC-1000 computer. One of this computer's most attractive features was its lack of need of maintenance. In fact, when you bought the computer, it came with a three-year money-back guarantee if the computer didn't perform properly. For three years and one month, the computer performed beautifully, but this morning your XC-1000 failed completely.

"One of the first things you did was have your assistant look for a newer replacement model which would perform the same functions. Unfortunately, as your company grew, all functions were built around your XC-1000, so you have very limited options. As a matter of fact, the lowest price replacement computer if you can't get a XC-1000 is $50,000.

"You made some tentative calls around the country of other firms that you knew bought XC-1000s. You discovered that most companies replaced them long ago. You were also a little concerned about buying a used model, since none were less than three years old, and the guarantee had expired.

"You called the president to apprise him of the problem, but his response was, 'Get another new XC-1000.' You called the manufacture of the XC-1000 and arranged a meeting with him tomorrow for an immediate purchase of an XC-1000. When you asked him the price, he told you there was one left and the price was negotiable. You began to prepare for your meeting.

"Do not reveal this information to individuals not on your team. Complete the answers to the following questions. You will have thirty minutes.

1. What price do you expect to pay for the XC-1000, and why?

2. What is the highest price you would pay, and why?

3. What is your strategy for your meeting tomorrow?"

Note that both sides in this situation have a problem. If the selling group does not sell the computer, they get absolutely nothing. If the buying group does not buy the computer, they must pay $50,000. Of course, at any price other than zero or $50,000, both negotiating sides gain. In fact, they might even benefit at these prices if there were other considerations. For example, the desire of the president of the copper tubing company for an XC-1000.

However, if we were calculating a fair price, we would probably agree that it would be the midpoint between zero and $50,000. That is, $25,000.

But remember, neither side has the information that the other has. Both know only of their own problem, and not the other side's.

Now, the interesting thing about this is that the prices vary widely between zero and $50,000 among different groups of buyers and sellers negotiating on the same day. Yet conditions are the same for all.

As I was writing this, I received a letter from Professor Steven W. McDaniel of Texas A & M University. He wrote to tell me that in one class the contract prices were $3,000, $10,000, and $2,500. A fourth team, which he noted was hard to believe, actually sold the computer at $55,000. This is even above the $50,000 that they would have to pay if they couldn't purchase an XC-1000!

From this exercise, students learn there isn't one single price for which a product must sell. Instead there are many prices that may completely satisfy a customer.

This little exercise also demonstrates something else. From the answers to my questions, I have found there is a direct relationship between the goals that they set and what they actually get. In other words, those teams that expect the best, get the best price. And it doesn't make any difference whether they are buyers or sellers, so long as they believe their price to be achievable.

General David C. Jones had an outstanding military career, and served as Chief-of-Staff of the Air Force, and later as Chairman of the Joint Chiefs of Staff. What are his views on leadership? General Jones cites another Air Force Chief of Staff, General Curtis Le May. General Le May built the Strategic Air Command into a major deterent force. "General Le May set very high standards for his command. Then he insisted that everyone meet those standards. General Le May said that over half of the Stategic Air Command would be on immediate alert at all times. Others said that this couldn't be done. But it was. Under Le May's leadership, safety, performance, and readiness reached unparelleled levels."[3]

John Sculley moved to Apple Computer after a brilliant career at Pepsi-Cola, where at thirty-eight he had been Pepsi-Cola's youngest president. Sculley encountered critical problems which culminated in the ousting from power of Steve Jobs, one of Apple's founders. Sculley planned new strategies, started the concept of desktop publishing, and motivated his salespeople to sell the new Macintosh computer. They sold enough to begin to make Apple profitable again. Did he tell them that they had achieved what he had intended? Here are his words from his book, *Odyssey:* "We have to raise our standards of excellence and I'm raising my expectations of what I want each of you to do. I'm proud of what you've done in the last month in turning the Macintosh around, but it's not time to relax."[4]

If you have high expectations in your leadership, you will find the same to be true. Who wins? Who are successful as leaders? Those with the highest expectations.

Maintain a Positive Attitude

Why didn't the British surrender to the Germans after France fell in the early days of World War II? Some say it was because of one man and one man only: Winston Churchill. In the early part of the war, the United States was not in the conflict and England stood alone. England was able to hold out against terrible odds because Winston Churchill had a positive attitude. This positive attitude helped make him determined to prevail.

Now, there is an interesting fact. Scientists have discovered that to a certain extent we can control our moods and feelings and maintain a positive attitude regardless of the reality of external facts. Famous psychologist and author of *Your Erroneous Zones* and many other books, Dr. Wayne Dyer has an interesting comment about external facts. He says, "It's not the facts that are important, but what you do with the facts and how you interpret them."

I said we could actually control how we feel. Let me demonstrate this to you right now. I would like you to read the next few paragraphs and then do what they request.

Wherever you are, I would like you to get as relaxed as you can. Then I would like you to close your eyes and relax even more.

Now, I would like you to imagine that there is a knock on the door. It is a special delivery for you. A distant uncle who you have never heard of has just died. You are his only living relative, and so he has left his entire fortune to you. This amounts to $1 million after taxes.

There are no conditions. You can do whatever you want to do with the money. You can buy anything you want. Put the money in the bank and live on the interest of $100,000 a year. Buy a yacht or an expensive car. Take a trip around the world. Or if you wish, you can give the entire amount or some part of it to your favorite charity. Many of the things that you always wanted to do are now possible.

While you continue to relax and with your eyes closed, imagine all the different things you are going to do with that $1 million. Are you going to take that vacation that you always wanted to take right now? Are you going to give money to that charity that you felt could help so many people? Are you going to buy that new sports car or wonderful home? Send your children to the best schools? What is it you want to do? Anything that you want will be yours because at least in your fantasy, you have actually received this check for $1 million tax-free.

Visualize all the things you will do with your $1 million. Visualize all the fun and satisfaction you will receive from doing them.

When you open your eyes, I want you to take note of your feelings. You will feel an increased sense of well being and happiness. Yet in reality nothing has changed. What has happened? What you have just done in this exercise is not only psychological. It is also physiological.

Norman Cousins demonstrated just how powerful this physiological effect is in his book *Anatomy of an Illness*. Norman Cousins cured himself of a death sentence from cancer. How did he do it? By locking himself up in a hotel room and repeatedly watching his favorite videos on television, those that made him laugh. He found that even though he was in pain, by watching several hours of video, he could get a few minutes' sleep.

As his worry left and his pain diminished, he got more and more sleep. Slowly his body began to heal itself. Eventually, the impossible happened. His body cured itself.

Norman Cousins had been the editor of *Saturday Review*. Today Cousins not only writes, but he lectures at a university. Because of his vital insights into the use of the mind for healing, the Dean of the UCLA Medical School appointed him to its faculty.

What is Cousins' secret? Cousins found that his body was actually a fully stocked drug store containing everything needed to heal his body. The key is in learning to use the mind to release the necessary drugs. Cousins did the same thing we did in our exercise of the million dollars.

The type of drugs we released in our exercise are endorphins. We released endorphins by fooling our subconscious mind into thinking something wonderful and unexpected happened. That we didn't actually receive $1 million was unimportant for our subconscious mind. It heard and saw that we had received $1 million. It knew that this should make us happy, and therefore released the endorphins to make this happen. This changed our perspective and gave us a more positive attitude. This more positive attitude existed regardless of anything else that might be happening around us at the time.

Scientists have conducted some interesting experiments with endorphins. You've probably heard about placebos. A placebo is a drug that works even though there is no reason for it to work. There may be nothing medically helpful in it, and yet the drug works anyway. Previously, scientists thought that this had to do with the patient's belief system. If the person believed strongly enough, the drug worked even though there was no reason for it to work.

Recently some medical research scientists suspected that this might have more to do with the release of endorphins. Their subjects were people subjected to frequent headaches. They divided their subjects into three groups. They told all their subjects there was a medicine whose efficacy in curing headaches they wanted to test.

Only one of these groups actually received a medicine. The second and third groups both received placebos—capsules containing ordinary tap water. However, the capsules taken by the third group did contain one other ingredient which blocked the endorphins from entering the bloodstream.

After the experiment, the results were tabulated. There wasn't too much difference between the headache relief received by the first and second groups. However, the third group that had their endorphins blocked from entering the bloodstream received a much lower incidence of headache relief. Thus, although positive thoughts or belief may have a psychological basis, there is a strong physiological dimension as well.

Dr. Dennis Waitley, the famous psychologist, is a graduate of the U.S. Naval Academy, a former member of the "Blue Angels" aerial acrobatic team, and the author of many books and tapes including *The Psychology of Winning*. He says: "If your friends ask if you are on drugs because of being so consistently positive, you can answer, 'Yes, endorphins.' To which they may respond, 'I always knew you were high on something.'"

Get Out in Front

There is only one real way to lead, and that is to get in front. You've got to lead by pulling and not pushing.

Admiral Wesley L. McDonald retired from his assignment as The Supreme Allied Commander, Atlantic, and the Commander in Chief of the U.S. Atlantic Command after having served in the U.S. Navy for over forty-two years. Speaking on leadership to a select group of senior officers from all services, Admiral McDonald gave his views on leadership: "Set the course—be the guy in front. If you do this, you'll be there when it counts . . . a foot in front every time."[5]

Did you know that the motto of both the Infantry School of the U.S. Army at Fort Benning, Georgia, and the Israeli Army is the same. It is: "Follow me."

Both mean what they say. The Israelis have a particularly no nonsense attitude toward combat leadership and getting out in front.

If you are an officer, you lead by physically being at the head of your troops. Now, this is somewhat contrary to the doctrine taught in the U.S. Army and many other armies around the world. Most armies say that to lead effectively, the commander should be with a forward unit, but not the most forward. If he's leading a patrol, he can be the number two man, but not the first. Why? Because if he is not at the front, he won't know what is going on. On the other hand, if he is all the way up front, he is more likely to become a casualty. That means a higher casualty rate of the scarce commodity of officer leaders.

The Israelis pay no mind to this and tell their officers: "If you are an officer, that's what you get paid for. You have to be in front of your men."

The Israelis have done this in every war that they've been in, and they have been at war with their neighbors since 1948. That they practice what they preach is confirmed by the fact that they have the highest officer casualty rate of any army in the world. Yet they do it anyway because they know that leaders must lead by getting out in front.

Being all the way at the front is not unique to the Israeli Army. During World War I, General Menoher, one of MacArthur's commanders, said: "I'm afraid we're going to lose him sometime, for there's no risk of battle that any soldier is called upon to take that he is not liable to look up and see MacArthur at his side. At every advance, MacArthur, with just his cap and his riding crop, will go forward with the first line. He is the source of the greatest possible inspiration to the men of his division who are devoted to him."[6]

No wonder MacArthur was promoted to Brigadier General when he was only thirty-eight.

Here again are six ways to make the combat model of leadership work for you:

1. Take risks. If you do so, you will eventually succeed. The turtle is able to move forward only by sticking his neck out. If you want to move forward as a leader, you must stick your neck out too.

2. Be innovative. There is more than one way to lead in any situation. Think before you act. See if you can't think of an effective way that hasn't been used before.

3. Take charge. Until you do, you can't lead. That doesn't mean that you must jump up and say, "I'm your leader." Actions speak louder than words. Take actions like General Grant did to get things moving.

4. Have expectations. The more you think your organization can accomplish, the more it will accomplish. Have the highest expectations of yourself and others and you can't fail.

5. Maintain a positive attitude. The world likes and is attracted to people with positive attitudes. Those that don't dwell on their problems. Instead, they think "can do," and then they do it.

6. Get out in front. You can't lead from behind.

Review these six ways to get the combat model to work for you every morning. Tell yourself that you are going to look for opportunities to implement them.

At the end of the day, review your actions. Note where you succeeded. In those instances where you fell short, replay the events in your mind and this time apply the concepts correctly. See the new outcome as a result of applying these concepts.

If you do this, in a short time you will be implementing the combat model without even thinking about it. The success you will achieve will be dramatic. So don't delay. Start thinking about ways in which you can apply these concepts today.

ENDNOTES

[1]Douglas MacArthur, *Reminiscences* (New York: McGraw-Hill Book Co., 1964), p. 70.

[2]The Armed Forces Officer (Washington, DC: The Department of Defense, 1950), p. 85.

[3]From a presentation to the Industrial College of the Armed Forces, Ft. McNair, Washington, DC, October 18, 1988.

[4]John Sculley with John A. Byrne, *Odyssey* (New York: Harper & Row, 1987), p. 332.

[5]From a presentation to students of the Industrial College of the Armed Forces, Ft. McNair, Washington, DC, October 25, 1988.

[6]Douglas MacArthur, op. cit., p. 70.

Chapter 3

FOUR WAYS TO GET PEOPLE TO FOLLOW YOU

No one follows anyone else without being motivated to do so. Look at any situation where men or women follow a leader, and you will discover reasons for their doing so. Luck or unusual circumstances may play a part, but mostly it is because of definite actions that the leader takes. In this chapter you will learn four actions that you must take to motivate others to follow you.

The Most Powerful Motivator of Human Behavior

Everyone wants to feel important, from the youngest child to the grandparent. After basic survival, it is one of the most important human needs. It is frequently the real reason behind both a child's tantrum and an adult's rudeness. A recent television special sought the reason that some children became school-ground bullies. Why do some children insist on dominating and threatening their playmates? Why do some children torment and persecute other children? Sociologists thought that bullies would be less intelligent. They thought that these would be the children who couldn't do well in class. In most cases, this just wasn't true.

What they did discover was that bullies got a sense of importance by lording over others. As one former bully, now grown up, told television viewers: "The more I was able to make weaker kids do what I wanted, the more important I felt."

But this same motivator can have a tremendously powerful effect. Toward the end of the Civil War, General Robert E. Lee faced a force of 100,000 Union troops with only 30,000 of his own. Just as he was about to be overrun, the Texas Brigade commanded by General John Gregg showed up.

As related by Alf J. Mapp, Jr., in his book *Frock Coats and Epaulets*, "Lee rode up to the front of the brigade, stood in his stirrups, raised his hat from his head and boomed above the martial din, 'Texans always move them.'

An ear-splitting yell rose from the brigade. One of Gregg's couriers, with tears running down his cheeks, shouted, 'I would charge hell itself for that old man!' " [1]

Making one feel important is more powerful as a motivator than money, promotion, working conditions, or almost anything else. So you just know that we do everything possible to make others feel important. Right? Wrong.

We do the exact opposite. When we meet a surly clerk, we don't think, "This person needs to feel important, and I'm going to make him or her feel that way." Oh no, not us! We think, "How dare this person talk that way to me. I'll show him how really unimportant he is compared with me."

So we play a game of one-upmanship in rudeness. The results are perfectly predictable. We have what is sometimes referred to in the military as a "pissing contest." We don't lead. We have a confrontation. If we have more power than the other person, we may get our way. But what about the future?

When you try to dominate rather than lead, you may or may not succeed. One thing, however, is certain. The person you are trying to dominate will not consider you his or her leader. You cannot trust that person to follow your lead in the future. In fact, if I had to bet some money, I would bet on the exact opposite.

The Woman Who Gives Away Pink Cadillacs

Experienced leaders know that making others feel important is crucial. Mary Kay Ash, the founder and CEO of Mary Kay Cosmetics, built a $300 million company starting with a $5,000 investment. You may not know of Mary Kay by name, but you may have heard of the woman who gives out pink Cadillacs to her most successful saleswomen. That's Mary Kay.

Several years ago, I was fortunate to be selected by the Direct Selling Association as one of a group of about twenty professors from all over the country to visit Mary Kay and her company. In 1985, we attended one of her annual sales meetings in Dallas, Texas. About 30,000 women attend these meetings each year, and I can vouch for the fact that it is a tremendous, motivating, and exciting experience.

To lead several hundred thousand saleswomen successfully, you have to be one heck of leader. Mary Kay is. She feels that making others feel important is so critical to the success of her business that she crafted a special technique to help her do this. What's Mary Kay's secret? Simply this. She imagines that every person she sees has a sign on his or her head. The sign reads: "Make me feel important." Mary Kay does everything she can to obey the sign's request.

How a General Made an Entire Air Force Feel Important

Four-star General Bill Creech became the commander of Tactical Air Command in the Air Force in 1978. Tactical Air Command, more familiarly known as TAC, includes over 100,000 "tigers." These are men and women who must be super aggressive in their work and ready to go to war at all times. Tom Peters and Nancy Austin reported what happened to TAC in their book, *A Passion for Excellence.*[2]

When General Creech took over TAC, the sortie rate had been falling over a ten-year period at a compound rate of 7.8 percent. A sortie is a flight mission by a single aircraft. The fact that the number of sorties launched every year was decreasing was not good. Further, when Creech arrived on the scene it took four hours for a spare part to get from inventory to an aircraft.

What was the situation when Creech left TAC in 1984? The sortie rate rose each year of Creech's tenure at a compound annual rate of 11.2 percent. Getting a part from inventory to the aircraft was no longer measured in hours. When Creech left, the average time was only eight minutes!

Now you may think that much of this was due to increased military budgets. Not so. The budget for spare parts actually decreased during this period.

How did Creech do it? Certainly Creech's success as a leader was because of the many things that he did, but making his people feel important was a major part.

He gave his support troops the importance they deserved: the same as he gave his pilots. He improved their housing, decorated their offices, and rewarded those who did well.

On one inspection tour in the west, he saw a supply sergeant's regulation Air Force chair that had a torn back and only three casters. Instead of the fourth caster, there was a brick. Electrical tape held the torn material in the back together.[3]

"Why don't you get a decent chair?" asked Creech.

"General, there aren't any available for supply sergeants right now."

"Sergeant, let me have your chair. I'll get a new one for you."

General Creech ordered his aide to fly the chair back to his headquarters at Langley Air Force Base, Virginia. He called in his three-star general in charge of logistics.

"General, I have a little present for you. It's a regulation Air Force chair, but its pretty beat up. It's yours until you get our logistic mess straightened out. And, oh yes . . . I need your old chair for a supply sergeant out west."

Supply sergeants were very important to the operations of TAC. By these actions, General Creech made this supply sergeant, and all supply sergeants, feel this importance. General Creech also showed his general in charge of logistics that he was very important . . . and in a very imaginative way.

So rule number one is this: if you want people to follow you, make them feel important.

How to Promote Your Vision

Leaders are not caretakers. They must have some idea as to where they want to go. It doesn't make any difference whether you are leader of a large Air Force Command of thousands of people, a softball team, or a small informal group. If you don't have any idea of where you are going, you can't get there. And neither can anyone else. As the Bible says, "Where there is no vision, the people perish" (Proverbs 24:18).

There is a strange insect called the Processionary Caterpillar. This insect bears this unusual name because of its unusual method of navigation. A number of Processionary Caterpillars will attach themselves front to back in a single line. The leader seeks the mulberry leaf, the main food of this caterpillar. Wherever the leader goes, the other Processionary Caterpillars are sure to follow. And off they go in this way, one continuous line of five or more caterpillars looking for mulberry leaves.

Several years ago a scientist conducted an experiment by taking a line of Processionary Caterpillars and formed them into a circle. What had been the leader was attached to what had been the last caterpillar in the line. Now there was no leader and no follower caterpillars. In the center of the circle of caterpillars he placed a bowl of mulberry leaves. The scientist wanted to know how long they would maintain the circle with no leader and no objective. He knew that eventually they must break the circle to eat the mulberry leaves or they would starve.

The result of this experiment surprised him. The caterpillars continued in a circle until they were so weak that they couldn't reach the mulberry leaves. Though food was only inches away, they continued to follow the caterpillar in front. They continued to go forward with no objective at all.

Men and women are not Processionary Caterpillars. If you have no vision of where you want to go, no one will follow you. Instead, your group will follow someone else who does know where he or she wants the group to go.

Professors Warren Bennis and Burt Nanus of the University of Southern California interviewed ninety leaders, including sixty successful CEOs and thirty outstanding leaders from the public sector. All ninety leaders had a well thought through vision of where they wanted their organizations to go. Bennis and Nanus termed the concern that these leaders had for their visions "unparalleled." Said Bennis and Nanus in their book, *Leaders*: "Their visions or intentions are compelling and pull people toward them."[4]

Four-star General Andrew J. Goodpaster, a confidant of presidents as well as former Supreme Allied Commander, Europe, puts what he calls: "Be clear about purpose," as his number one principle of leadership.[5]

William G. McGowan, founder and CEO of the billion dollar MCI Communications Corporation, is the man who cracked the long-distance monopoly of American Telephone and Telegraph Company. McGowan firmly believes, "People don't come to MCI for security. They come to be challenged, to be part of something new."[6]

People are attracted to a leader's vision and future goals because they recognize that through them, they and the organization can become permanently better.

Major General Perry M. Smith, former Commandant of the National War College in Washington, D.C., found that, "A leader can permanently affect an organization by establishing a strategic

vision and setting long-term goals."[7] Four-star General Edward
C. Meyer, former Chief of Staff of the army, a man who helped to
permanently change the organization of the Joint Chiefs of Staffs,
says that without vision, organizations will fail.

Vision is clearly pretty important, but having an objective of
where you want the organization to go is only half the action you
must take. The other half is to insure that others know what your
vision is. By communicating your vision you get a consensus
among those you lead.

President John Young of Hewlett-Packard said: "Successful
companies have a consensus from top to bottom on a set of overall
goals. The most brilliant management strategy will fail if that
consensus is missing."[8]

James E. Buerger, publisher of *Travelhost National* magazine, set
up his own printing plant by following this principle. He had just
forty-five days after ordering a press to raise $100,000, set up his
equipment, get trained operators, and find a building to house
everything. He did it by communicating his goals effectively after
setting them. According to Buerger, "A secret goal cannot benefit
from the participation and force of others. A well-defined goal,
shared with others and sparked with enthusiasm, will draw energy and forces that cannot be measured or suppressed."[9]

If you have a vision and communicate it to others, you will
succeed though the odds are against you.

You Can Promote Your Vision Anywhere

Colonel Julian Ewell, commanding the 501st Parachute Infantry
Regiment, reached Bastogne, Belgium, on the night of December
18, 1944. Two days earlier, the Germans had begun their Ardennes
campaign. This was the Germans last major offensive of World
War II, and history tells us it was a very close thing. Ewell arrived
with only one battalion of less than a 1,000 men. Higher headquarters couldn't tell him the enemy's situation . . . the friendly
situation . . . nothing.

But Ewell had a vision and he communicated it to his men.
"We're going to attack the Germans." They did. In so doing, they
stopped the German 27th Panzer Corps of more than 30,000 troops
dead in its tracks. It forced Hitler to change his Ardennes plan and
may have altered the course of World War II.[10]

Roger Ailes, a communications consultant who has consulted
for a number of CEOs and political campaigns, says that, ". . . the
essence of charisma is showing your commitment to an idea or

goal."[11] Of course showing commitment to an idea or goal is the same as vision. Behavioral scientists have found a close correlation between communicating vision and being perceived as charismatic.

Martin Luther King Jr., one of the most charismatic leaders of our time, said, "I have a vision."

If you want others to follow you, you must have a vision too, and you must communicate it to others.

Treat Others as You Would Be Treated Yourself and They Will Follow Your Lead

Both the Old and New Testaments tell us to treat others as we want to be treated ourselves. You may have thought this concept has application only in religion or the practice of ethical conduct. The truth is it also has a great deal to do with good leadership. Why? Because people do not willingly follow leaders who are unconcerned with how they are treated.

Mary Kay Ash calls this her "Golden Rule System of Management." She not only practices it herself, but recommends it to everyone who leads.

After all, what makes you so special? Do you think that you are so much better than others that you are to be treated differently? If you do, better change your way of thinking, or you may never get people to follow you.

What We Learned from the Largest Leadership Study Ever Done

During World War II, the U.S. Army gathered together sixty-one of the greatest authorities in the field of psychology to prepare and publish a special study. They came from some of the most prestigious universities in the country. Harvard, Yale, Brown, the University of Pennsylvania, and many others were represented. When they were done, their research was published under the title *Psychology for the Fighting Man*.

One of their studies was especially unique. For the first time in the history of armies, enlisted soldiers were interviewed about what they thought about good leadership. Want to know what these thousands of soldiers thought made good leaders? The number one factor by frequency of response was "competence." The good officer was expected to know his stuff.

That answer was pretty much expected. What was not expected had to do with the next fourteen most frequently cited factors. The second, fourth, sixth, and seventh most frequent responses all had to do with treatment. These were:

- interest in the welfare of the soldier (second)
- patience and ability to make things clear (fourth)
- doesn't boss you around without reason (sixth)
- tells you when you did a good job (seventh)

The soldiers interviewed gave these responses more frequently than "physical strength" (eighth), "good education" (ninth), or even "guts" (eleventh).[12]

The Armed Forces Officer, a book on leadership written for officers in all of our armed services says:

"Though it has been said before, even so, it can be said again: It is a paramount and overriding responsibility of every officer to take care of his men before caring for himself. . . . *It is a cardinal principle!* If an officer is on a tour with an enlisted man, he takes care that the man is accommodated as to food, shelter, medical treatment or other prime needs, before satisfying his own wants; if that means that the last meal or the last bed is gone, his duty is to get along the hard way."[13]

We had a saying at West Point that a leader should be "hard, but fair." So if you want others to follow you, treat them fairly. Treat them as you would like to be treated yourself, and put the welfare of those you lead before your own welfare.

Take Responsibility for Your Actions and Admit Your Mistakes

As a leader, you will be taking the responsibility for attaining an objective. That objective may be one set by a higher organization than the one you are in. It could be an objective set by your followers. Or it could be an objective you set for yourself. Who sets the objective is unimportant.

The size of the group isn't important either. It could be a group of hundreds of thousands, or it could be you and one other person. Once you take on the leadership of a group, you and you alone are responsible for reaching the objective.

You can delegate to others that you lead the *authority* to do certain tasks, but you cannot delegate responsibility. It doesn't make any difference whether those that follow you perform well or poorly, or even if they carry out the instructions you have given them.

Of course, you should take responsibility and admit your mistakes. It's the right thing to do. Beyond being the right thing, it is the only thing to do if you want to be a leader. Do, and those you lead will give you their trust and follow you anywhere. Fail to do this and you will not be a leader for very long.

Andrew S. Grove is President and Chief Executive Officer of the Intel Corporation. This company, built largely through the efforts of Grove, is not only a "Fortune 500" company, but is also listed in *The 100 Best Companies to Work for in America*. Yet, *Fortune* magazine calls Andy Grove one of the ten toughest bosses in America to work for. What does Grove say about taking responsibility and admitting mistakes? Let's listen to him.

"All of us in management (and in teaching, government, even parenting)—men and women, young or old—worry about losing hard-won respect by admitting our mistakes. Yet, in reality, admitting mistakes is a sign of strength, maturity, and fairness."[14]

The amazing John Sculley, President of Apple Computer, says the same thing: "Making mistakes is a very real and important part of succeeding. At Apple, making mistakes is the only way to learn. If you fail to convey the idea at the top that you can make mistakes, you can send the wrong message, isolate yourself from the people."[15]

Why Did Men Follow Robert E. Lee?

Robert E. Lee is probably the most beloved military leader in U.S. history. Not only to the day of his death, but until years afterward, those who knew him or served under him revered his name. Even his former enemies honored him and flocked to visit him after the Civil War. Here he was, the most notorious defeated enemy general of the Confederacy, and yet company presidents from New York offered him hundreds of thousands of dollars if he would associate with their companies. He turned them all down. Instead he accepted a post as president of a small college in Virginia with only forty students.

Lee had not won the war. He had been forced to surrender his Army of Northern Virginia to General Grant. The best chance that the Confederacy had to win the Civil War was the Battle of Gettysburg in July 1863. Lee lost that decisive battle.

Sure, Lee had plenty of plenty of bad luck and the poor performance of some of his generals on which to blame his loss.

Lee's famous "strong right arm," "Stonewall" Jackson, had been killed at the Battle of Chancellorsville a few months earlier. His brilliant young cavalry leader, Jeb Stuart, went off on his own and didn't appear on the battlefield until the last day. As a result, Lee had very little intelligence about the Union forces he faced. Lieutenant General Ewell who commanded part of Jackson's old corps could have won the battle for Lee the first day. All he had to do was to occupy a deserted, but strategically important hill. He failed to do so.

Lee's second in command, General Longstreet, strongly opposed a charge ordered by Lee to be made by one of his divisions commanded by Major General Pickett. As a result he failed to give Pickett positive orders. Preparations took longer than they should have. The charge was not coordinated with a diversionary attack as previously planned.

Pickett's troops were fully exposed to the murderous effect of enemy guns and direct fire. Only a few hundred of his troops even managed to reach Union lines. Of the 13,000 Confederates who made the charge, more than 7,000 were left dead or wounded in "no man's land" between the two lines.

With the battle clearly lost, and the remnants of Pickett's men returning to the Confederate lines, it was Lee that went out to meet the survivors.

"It was all my fault and no one else's," he said. "You did your best, but it was I who failed you."

In tears, these battle-weary soldiers shouted: "No! No! You didn't fail, General. It was us."

Robert E. Lee always took responsibility for his actions, and his men loved him for it and fought all the harder. Remember that the Battle of Gettysburg was in early July 1863. Lee didn't surrender his army at Appomattox Court House until April 1865 . . . almost two years later.

Why a Squadron Commander Who Was Never There Was Reported for Being Drunk

As a leader, you and you alone are responsible for everything that those who follow you do, or fail to do. Hap Arnold, who was the five-star Commanding General of the Army Air Force during World War II, illustrates this in his book *Army Flyer*.[16] A new squadron commander received a message from his group commander. "You drank too much at the Officer's Club last night. Don't let it happen again."

Now the problem was that this young officer had never been at the Officer's Club on the night in question. Shrugging it off, he decided to do nothing.

Several days later, he received another message. "You drank too much again. This is your final warning."

Now this new squadron commander was really puzzled, because he hadn't been at the club on that night either. This time, however, he called the deputy group commander to talk it over.

The deputy group commander understood the situation perfectly. "Major, you're not responsible for just yourself anymore. You're now responsible for the actions of everyone in your squadron. You personally weren't drinking too much at the Officer's Club. But one of the members of your squadron was. You're responsible!"

Two Unwanted Outcomes That Are Easily Avoided

Now I know that you may think this a bit strong. How can you be responsible for everything that someone does who happens to be in your organization? In the military, you are responsible because you have a twenty-four-hour-a-day job and have authority over those you lead twenty-four hours a day.

The problem is that many leaders of nonmilitary organizations simply don't take responsibility for the actions of their charges under any circumstances. You can always find excuses for failing, but then two undesirable results will be achieved.

First, those who follow you will not want you to be their leader. Would you if you were them? After all, the contract is leadership in exchange for responsibility. When you don't take responsibility for the group you lead, you violate this contract.

The second unwanted result will come from whoever you report to. Your boss wants to know that he or she can rely on you. If you aren't responsible for your organization, then who is? Who is it that your boss can rely on?

You can't delegate responsibility, so don't try. When things go wrong, think of General Lee and say, "It was all my fault and no one else's."

Four Action Steps to Get People to Follow You

1. Make others feel important. People will follow you when you make them feel important, not when you make yourself feel important.

2. Promote your vision. No one will follow you simply because you decide you want to lead. You have to have a clear idea of where you want to take the group— then you must promote it to your group and convince them that your goal is worthwhile.

3. Treat others as you would be treated yourself. This is so basic, why don't we do it more often? After all, would you want to follow someone who treated you poorly? Don't you prefer to follow leaders who have concern for you and your feelings and treat you well? So do those who would follow you.

4. Take responsibility for your actions and those of your group. Admit your mistakes. You are responsible for everything the members of your group do or fail to do. So when things go wrong, don't forget to accept this responsibility. If you try to foster this responsibility off on others, you are no longer the leader.

Take the time to digest these four ways to get people to follow you. Then proceed to the next chapter for three additional things that you must do.

ENDNOTES

[1] Alf J. Mapp, Jr. *Frock Coats and Epaulets* (Hamilton Press: New York, 1987), p. 203.

[2] Tom Peters and Nancy Austin, *A Passion for Excellence* (New York: Random House, 1985), p. 48.

[3] *Ibid.*, p. 275.

[4] Warren Bennis and Burt Nanus, *Leaders* (New York: Harper and Row, 1985), p. 28.

[5] From a presentation to students of the Industrial College of the Armed Forces at Ft. McNair, Washington, DC, November 8, 1988.

[6] John Wilke, "McGowan: The Man Who Cracked AT&T," *Business Week* (January 21, 1985), p. 69.

[7] Perry M. Smith, *Taking Charge* (Washington, DC: National Defense University Press, 1986), p. xvii.

[8] Jonathan Carr, "Success as a State of Mind," *Financial Times* (February 13, 1984).

[9] Charles Garfield, *Peak Performers* (New York: Avon, 1986), pp. 121–22.

[10] *The Armed Forces Officer* (Washington, DC: U.S. Government Printing Office, 1950), pp. 136–37.

[11] Roger Ailes, "The Secret of Charisma," *Success* (July/August 1988), p. 14.

[12] Committee of the National Research Council with the collaboration of Science Service, *Psychology for the Fighting Man* (Washington, DC/New York: Infantry Journal/Penguin Books, 1944), pp. 306–307.

[13] *The Armed Forces Officer* (Washington, DC: U.S. Government Printing Office, 1950), pp. 28–29.

[14] Andrew S. Grove, *One-On-One with Andy Grove* (New York: G.P. Putnam's Sons, 1987), p. 60.

[15] John Sculley with John A. Byrne, *Odyssey* (New York: Harper & Row, 1987), p. 333.

[16] Henry H. Arnold and Ira Eaker, *Army Flyer* (New York: Harper, 1942).

Chapter 4

THREE ADDITIONAL WAYS TO ATTRACT FOLLOWSHIP

In this chapter, we're going to examine three additional ways which will encourage others to follow your lead. The first simply requires a readjustment of the way you do things. You must praise in public and criticize in private. Unfortunately, many leaders fail to do this. As a result, they are resented. In addition, they fail to take full advantage of the opportunity that accomplishment represents. These leaders rarely reach their maximum potential.

Seeing and being seen and using competition as a motivator are two tools you shouldn't be without. Their use will not only help in getting others to follow you, but will aid in your perception as being positively charismatic.

Why You Must Praise in Public, Criticize in Private

No one likes to be told that they did something wrong. We all like to think that we do things right, even though we know this is not always true. When we do something really wrong, our feelings are even stronger. Even if no one else is there, the person who criticizes us must be careful. Otherwise, this criticism could cause us to react strongly against the critic.

Sometimes, we must tell someone that we lead that he or she did something wrong. When we do this we must do this in a special way. I will show you this way shortly.

If you really want to make enemies and make your job of leadership difficult, just tell someone that he or she did something wrong in front of others. You will embarrass the person you criticize. Not only will this person not want to follow you, you may never be forgiven! If the others present happen to support the person you criticize, you may make even more enemies. So don't do it!

On the other hand, everyone likes praise. And when we receive praise, we'd like everyone to know about it. So the simple secret is, praise in public, but criticize in private.

Now both of these concepts are crucial. You must let people know how they are doing. You want them to know what they did that was wrong so they won't do it again. But recognizing when someone does something right is equally important. And you want them to know what they did that was right so they will do it again.

Kenneth Blanchard and Spencer Johnson, coauthors of *The One Minute Manager*, feel that the second element of this concept is so important that they gave it a special name. They call it "catching someone doing something right."[1]

How to Minimize Negative Reactions to Criticism

Okay, so you are going to criticize only in private. How can you do it to minimize the chance of a negative reaction? It's easy. Just say something good about the person at the same time.

Mary Kay goes one better. She recommends saying two good things about the person you are criticizing, before and after. She calls this her "sandwich technique."

How does it work? Let's say that you must criticize someone you lead because they are late fifteen to twenty minutes in getting to work every morning.

First you find two things that this person does well. Let's say that this person writes very good reports, and is always on time in providing them to you.

Since the purpose of the meeting is to criticize, you talk to him in private. You start with something he does right.

"Joe, you are doing a great job with your reports. They are always accurate and well organized. The advice you give us is a tremendous help in our marketing effort."

Now you put the meat in your sandwich. That's the criticism:

"Joe, we also need your advice every morning. Your coming to work fifteen to twenty minutes late every morning is hurting us.

Sometimes I or others need you because a customer on the east coast calls us. We have to make the decision without your advice, and we don't always guess right. We need you here on time every morning. That's what I expect from now on."

Finally, you complete the sandwich by adding the other thing that Joe does well. "You know because you are always on time with your reports, I rely on your advice in them completely. I couldn't do nearly as well without you, and neither could our organization."

Notice how the criticism is sandwiched in between two compliments. This takes the sting out and lets "Joe" keep his self-respect. He knows that he is important to you and to the organization. He also knows that you want him at work on time.

Robert E. Lee's Most Difficult Criticism

General Robert E. Lee didn't use the sandwich technique, but he did understand the importance of giving strong praise along with strong criticism.

Remember the Battle of Gettysburg and how Lee's cavalry commander, Jeb Stuart, failed to provide information on the Union forces? Lee could have fired Stuart. Some commanders in the Army of Northern Virginia thought that Jeb Stuart should be court-martialed. But Lee would have lost a great cavalry commander. Still, Lee could not let Stuart's action pass without criticism. Had he done this, Stuart might have repeated it in the future. Jeb Stuart, though a lieutenant general, was high strung. He was only thirty years old. If Lee was not careful in his criticism, Stuart might resign from the army anyway. Here's how General Robert E. Lee handled the situation.

"You were my eyes. Your mission was to screen this army from the enemy cavalry and to report any movement by the enemy's main body. That mission was not fulfilled."

Stuart stood motionless.

Lee said, "You left this army without word of your movements, or of the movements of the enemy, for several days. We were forced into battle without adequate knowledge of the enemy's position, or strength, without knowledge of the ground. It is only by God's grace that we have escaped disaster."

"General Lee." Stuart was in pain, and the old man felt pity, but this was necessary; it had to be done as a bad tooth has to be pulled, and there was no turning away. Yet even now he felt pity rise, and he wanted to say, it's all right, boy, it's all right; this is only a lesson, just one painful quick moment of learning, over in a moment, hold on, it'll be all right. His voice began to soften. He could not help it.

"It is possible that you misunderstood my orders. It is possible that I did not make myself clear. Yet this must be clear: you with your cavalry are the eyes of the army. Without your cavalry we are blind, and that has happened once but must never happen again."

There was a moment of silence. It was done. Lee wanted to reassure him, but he waited, giving it time to sink in, to take effect, like medicine. Stuart stood breathing audibly. After a moment he reached down and unbuckled his sword, theatrically, and handed it over with high drama in his face. Lee grimaced, annoyed, put his hands behind his back, half turned his face. Stuart was saying that since he no longer held the General's trust, but Lee interrupted him with acid vigor.

"I have told you that there is no time for that. There is a fight tomorrow, and we need you. We need every man, God knows. You must take what I have told you and learn from it, as a man does. There has been a mistake. It will not happen again. I know your quality. You are a good soldier. You are as good a cavalry officer as I have known, and your service to this army has been invaluable. I have learned to rely on your information; all your reports are always accurate. But no report is useful if it does not reach us. And that is what I wanted you to know. Now." He lifted a hand, "Let us talk no more of this."[2]

If you want others to do what you say, praise in public, criticize in private. And combine your criticism with praise.

Why You Must See and Be Seen

I don't care who you are leading. You can't lead from behind a desk. In the four months before the allied invasion of Europe during World War II, General Eisenhower visited twenty-six divisions, twenty-four airfields, five war ships, and numerous military bases, depots, hospitals, and many other military installations. All of his senior subordinates maintained similar visiting schedules. He said, "There is among the mass of individuals who carry the rifles in war, a great amount of ingenuity and initiative. If men can naturally and without restraint talk to their officers, the products of their resourcefulness become available to all."[3] Eisenhower said that this promoted, "Mutual confidence, a feeling of partnership that is the essense of esprit de corps."[4]

You've got to see those that you lead yourself, and let them see you. Robert W. Galvin, Chairman of the Board and Chief Executive Officer of Motorola, Inc., says: "I believe we in top management must circulate."[5]

Tom Peters, who I told you about earlier believes this because he found seeing and being seen is an action taken by effective leaders in every successful company and organization he visited. As a result, Peters formalized the technique and gave it a name. He calls it MBWA, "management by wandering around."

If it weren't for MBWA, General Creech may never have discovered the supply problems that he had when he took over TAC. He certainly could never have communicated his ideas so effectively. When you have a supply sergeant's chair exchanged for the chair of one of your generals, the news gets around!

And maybe that's the idea. When you go out and see and are seen by those you lead, you greatly increase the effectiveness of communications up and down the chain of command. You find out what's right and what's wrong in your organization. And you can correct things instantly. You can dramatize your ideas to your followers. That way the word gets around . . . fast.

How General Patton Led by Seeing and Being Seen

As commander of the Third Army, General George S. Patton practiced MBWA. He found that his soldiers didn't always wear their heavy steel helmets. The helmet was an important factor for survival. More important was the implied lack of battlefield discipline, since wearing of the helmet was required in combat by army regulations. Other things Patton saw also convinced him that discipline wasn't what it should be. Lack of discipline in combat cost lives and lost battles.

Patton took instant action to correct the situation. He issued orders that any soldier not wearing his steel helmet *and a tie* would be court-martialed.

Combat dress etiquette dictates that officers be indistinguishable from the soldiers they lead. Otherwise, they could be singled out as targets by the enemy. Patton not only wore a helmet and tie, but fixed his jeep with flying flags. He wore a revolver on one hip and an automatic on the other. No one could mistake Patton on the battlefield, and his visits were legendary. His seeing and being seen helped make him a successful battlefield commander.

While in Israel in 1972, I met another man who believes in seeing and being seen. A General Electric vice president, he was helping the Israelis with their General Electric built J-79 engines. This man is an American by the name of Gerhardt Neuman.

Neuman was a refugee from Nazi Germany. During World War II, he was in charge of maintenance for General Chanault's Flying Tigers in China.

Neuman had a problem with engine reliability. The engines of the P-40s which Chanault's flyers flew worked well enough on the ground. In the air it was another story. Sometimes they faltered just when needed during combat against the Japanese.

In other airplanes, a ground crewman could fly in the airplane to investigate the problem. But the P-40 was a fighter with a single seat. There was no space for anyone else. So Neuman's groundcrews couldn't find the problem.

But Neuman believed in management by wandering around, or in this case management by flying around. He worked out a means by which he flew sitting in the pilot's lap. This method worked so well that it became the way all test flights were conducted. Soon all of Neuman's maintenance men checked out their aircraft's engine in this way.

One of Neuman's managers told me that Neuman's workers always came to work early no matter what job they had or where they worked. The reason was that Neuman always seemed to be on the spot earlier to greet them. It became a game. Neuman's people wanted to be at work early enough to greet him rather than be greeted.

You Must Know Who Your People Really Are

When you go out to see and be seen you not only learn what's going on, you learn who your people really are. A person isn't just a number with certain skills who is paid a certain amount of money and has certain seniority in your organization. A person is a man or woman of flesh and blood. He or she has a wife or husband, girlfriend or boyfriend, children, hopes, dreams, problems, victories, defeats, opportunities, and so on. Is it any wonder that leadership is complex? That a person may follow you in one situation and not in another?

To lead successfully, you must see every single one of those who would follow you as an individual. For a start, while going out and seeing and being seen, you can learn the names of those you lead. It doesn't really matter how large an organization you lead. They say that Julius Caesar knew the names of thousands of his legionnaires. He called them by name, and they won battles for him.

Surely if you expect those who follow you to know your name, they will expect no less of you. Learn the names of those you lead because they deserve it. Learn them because it will help you to get to know them. Learn their names because it will make your seeing and being seen even more effective. Douglas D. Danforth, Chairman of the Board at the Westinghouse Corporation, says: "The better the CEO knows his key people personally, the better he will be able to correctly estimate their strengths."[6]

So if you lead a large organization, you can at least learn the names of those you lead. And if you lead a smaller organization, how fortunate you are! You can learn much more about those who follow you. And the more you know, the more you will see and understand. The better you will know their strengths and weaknesses. The more others will understand what you want and how this fits into the organization's goals and objectives.

What if you are having problems with those you are leading? Isn't it better to stay out of the way for awhile? Shouldn't you avoid the chance of a direct confrontation? Management experts have discovered that even when you expect opposition, face-to-face communications improve the likelihood of understanding. When there are disagreements between you and those you lead, you should see and be seen as you have never done so before.[7]

How Cortez Succeeded by Facing Up to His Problems

Cortez, the Spanish Conqueror of Mexico, was faced with a general revolt. Many of his troops, including his leading commanders thought that he had gone too far and risked too much. They wanted to return to their ships and sail back to Spain.

Cortez didn't avoid the problem. He sought out the rebels in their own place of meeting. There was a general murmur of disapproval on his arrival. "This doesn't concern you," one shouted. "We don't want to die for your glory," said another.

Cortez ignored the disrespect and began to speak. "It is true there is great risk in what we do, and no man need be ashamed because he wants to go home. I want to go home myself. But we are under orders of the crown to explore and conquer this land.

So I must stay until these tasks are complete. But perhaps you do not. Not every man has the courage to be a conqueror or an explorer. Those who possess such courage win wealth and fame. But not every man needs to win wealth and fame. Let us decide here and now whether you have the courage to win wealth and fame or will return home now."

Cortez drew his sword and scratched a straight line in the dirt floor between himself and the would-be rebels.

"All those who are men who have the courage to win wealth and fame cross over to my side of the line," he said. "The others may return to the ships."

To a man, all crossed over, and this was the last time Cortez's leadership was questioned.

By seeing and being seen, you can:

> • know what's going on in your organization every day
> • help those who need help
> • get help from those who can supply help
> • discover the real problems
> • uncover opportunities you didn't know existed
> • praise and recognize those that deserve it
> • correct or discipline those that need it
> • get your word out fast
> • communicate your vision for the organization
> • insure everyone understands your goals and objectives

Seeing and being seen sounds like a pretty simple action to take. It is. But by this simple action you will accomplish all of the above and others will follow where you lead.

How to Use Competition to Make Striving a Game

Have you participated in a competitive sport? If not, I'm sure that you have at least watched one. Competitive sports include everything from golf to football, from boxing to gymnastics. Competitive sports can be rough, fast or slow, or require great skill, endurance, or knowledge. They can be played on the ground, above the ground, on ice, in water, or underwater. They can involve balls, rackets, carts, chariots, guns, cars, airplanes, boats, skis, skates, or ships. One ancient sport actually involved vaulting over live bulls.

Whatever the sport or the manner of its playing, all involve competition with one or more other human beings. The competition makes the sport exciting and fun. Competitive sports are not work, they are play. As a result, while work tires us, we can play at competitive sports on and on.

In this fact lies a secret that all of us can use to make the task that we want to do fun, rather than work. All you have to do is make striving a game. Not possible with your kind of task you say? Let me assure you that it's possible with any task.

Let me tell you first that in competition lies the secrets of setting records in everything in life. Records are set not on practice fields, but in real competition such as the Olympics.

At one time it was thought that competition brought too much pressure to bear in learning. So a change was made. Students no longer received grades. Instead, their only grades were pass or fail. Educators thought this would improve performance in the classroom and also in real learning. The idea was that instead of "wasting time" competing, students would be learning. What happened? The exact opposite. Not only did students participate to a lesser extent in the classroom, but objective tests proved that students didn't learn as much.

Scientists tell us that there are two types of stress caused by pressure. One is the bad kind of stress. It is overwhelming and causes performance to fall off. Competition, however, is the good kind of stress. In most cases, it causes a performance increase.

How Eddie Rickenbacher Used Competition To Help Shoot Down Planes

Eddie Rickenbacher shot down twenty-six enemy airplanes to become our "Ace of Aces" during World War I. One day his commander was killed in action. Rickenbacher became commander of the 94th Aero Squadron in France.

Combat losses were heavy. Worse yet, many pilots were being killed in noncombat aircraft crashes because of maintenance problems. The squadron was dependent on equipment provided by the French as American airplanes weren't available. The pilots felt that they were not getting the best equipment. Morale was extremely low. At this point Rickenbacher was made squadron commander.

"First I called the pilots together," he said. "I pointed out that our airplanes were the same as other squadrons at the front, including the French. I asked them whether they felt that the French were better pilots. When they indicated that they felt that the 94th Aero Squadron had the best pilots at the front, I challenged them to prove it by a competition with the other fighter squadrons. It was simple to keep score. Whichever squadron shot the most planes down was the winner.

"Next I called a meeting of all our groundcrews. I noted that without them, the pilots might just as well stay on the ground. I told them about the competition the pilots were in with the other combat squadrons. While they were part of this competition, I challenged them to compete with the other squadron groundcrews. This competition was in number of aircraft fit for flight and in accidents because of maintenance.

"I knew from my racing days that competition works . . . that men will work harder when the goal is to beat someone else . . . even if it is a friend."

It goes without saying that under Rickenbacher's leadership the 94th Aero Squadron became the best American squadron in the war. And Rickenbacher used the same technique to build Eastern Airlines from nothing to one of the best run airlines of his time.

If you want people to follow you, show them the competition and make your task a game. They'll follow your lead and make your organization a winner.

Three Actions to Take Whenever You Can

1. Praise in public, criticize in private. If people have earned your praise, let everyone know about it. Encourage others to earn praise also. If you have something to criticize, do it. But do it in private. Don't embarrass people unnecessarily. Frequently just the fact that you are displeased is embarrassment enough.

2. Take the time to see and be seen. You've got to get around to really know what's going on, to fix what's wrong, and to capitalize on what's going right. At the same time, you want to be seen. This provides additional opportunities to talk with and motivate everyone in your group. And you can be sure that you will gain secondary motivation. "When I was talking with the boss yesterday" is a phrase that will be repeated frequently.

3. Use competition to make striving a game. People love to compete. That's one of the secrets of successful products from professional sports to video games. You can make competition a positive force to reach your objectives.

When you complete this chapter, you will be ready for the influence strategies in the next two chapters. Mastering them will give you new ways for maximizing the potential in a wide variety of situations which require your leadership.

ENDNOTES

[1] Kenneth Blanchard and Spencer Johnson, *The One-Minute Manager* (New York: William Morrow, 1982).

[2] Quoted from Michael Shaara, *The Killer Angels* (New York: Ballantine Books, 1974), pp. 266–266. Used with permission.

[3] Edgar F. Puryear, *19 Stars: A Study in Military Character and Leadership* (Presidio, CA: Presidio Press, 1971), pp. 229–230.

[4] Dwight D. Eisenhower, *Crusade in Europe* (New York: Doubleday and Co., Inc., 1948), p. 314.

[5] Chester Burger, *The Chief Executive* (Boston: CBI Publishing Co., Inc., 1978), p. 48.

[6] Jerome M. Rosow, "A View from the Top," *Success* (February 1986), p. 69.

[7] James M. Kouzes and Barry Z. Posner, "The Leadership Challenge," *Success* (April 1988, p. 69).

Chapter 5

HOW TO LEAD ANYONE USING THE FOUR BASIC INFLUENCE STRATEGIES

We lead others by influencing them. Sometimes this influence is accidental. When this happens, we may find that we have led others to a goal successfully with no conscious effort. Experienced leaders may also influence others successfully below their own level of consciousness. However, you cannot learn to lead this way, and even experienced leaders can frequently lead better by consciously planning their strategies.

Leading Below the Level of Consciousness

Leading below the level of consciousness is like driving a car. When we first learn to drive, we must consciously think about every single move that we make. We must think not only about pushing and pulling on buttons, levers, and pedals, but also navigating the vehicle to where we want to go in accordance with good driving practice and the law. In addition, we must think about avoiding collision with people, obstacles, and other vehicles.

Eventually everything becomes automatic and we don't have to think much about driving at all. We can successfully operate the car while thinking about work, carrying on a conversation with others, listening to the radio, or even learning a language on tape. We may get where we are going and not even remember turning the ignition on!

Once you are an experienced leader, or if you already are, you may not need to consciously think about influencing others. Like driving a car, you are "on automatic."

However, no one should rely on luck or accident for success in leadership. Also, even as an experienced leader (or driver) there are a significant number of situations where you cannot operate "on automatic." This is when you must consciously use your skill and apply the influence strategies.

More Reasons You Must Know and Apply
the Influence Strategies

Understanding the influence strategies are important for two other reasons. First, leadership is not limited to leading those who formally report to you. Sometimes you must lead colleagues. At other times, you must even lead those to whom you report.

An understanding of the influence strategies is also important because their use must vary according to the situation and who you want to influence. In some cases one influence strategy is appropriate, and it will work wonders and enable your success. In a slightly different circumstance the exact same influence strategy will guarantee failure 100 times out of 100.

A German combat leader from World War I described a classical example of influence strategies used in 1917 by a brigade commander.

Describing his three regimental commanders, the brigade commander said that his first regimental colonel wanted to do everything himself, and always did well. His second colonel executed every order, but had no initiative. Finally, there was the commander of his third regiment. He opposed everything he was told, and always wanted to do the contrary.

A few days later, the brigade came up against a heavily defended position that had to be attacked. The brigade commander issued different orders to each regimental commander.

To his first colonel he said: "My dear Colonel 'A,' I think we will attack. Your regiment will have to carry the burden of the attack. I have, however, selected you for this reason. The second regiment will be your boundary on the left. The third regiment will be your boundary on the right. Attack at 1200 hours. I don't have to tell you anything more."

To his third colonel who opposed everything, the brigade commander spoke quite differently. "We have met a very strong enemy. I am afraid we will not be able to attack with the forces at our disposal."

As he knew would happen, his third colonel didn't agree.

"Oh, General, certainly we will attack. Just give my regiment the time of attack and you will see that we will be successful."

"Go, then, we will try it," said the brigade commander and he gave him the formal order for the attack which he had prepared previously.

As for the commander of his second regiment, he simply sent the attack order with more details than he had given his other commanders.

All three regiments attacked successfully.[1]

In this chapter you will learn the four strategies and how to apply them in practice over a wide variety of situations and leadership roles. Your proper use of the four influence strategies will equip you with the arsenal to make you a powerful leader.

Pamela C. Cuming, President of Dialectics, Inc., an organizational consulting firm, and a woman who has done remarkable work on the influence strategies, says: "People who manage power properly do so in a way that inspires the commitment and/or cooperation of others. They perceive power not as an end in itself, but as a means to an end."[2]

The Four Basic Influence Strategies

What are the four basic influence strategies? Here they are:

1. Persuasion
2. Negotiation
3. Involvement
4. Direction

As we will see, not only are all of these influence strategies usable, but all are needed to properly lead under the many different conditions a leader faces.

When and How a Leader Must Use Persuasion to Lead

Did you think that a leader always has a great deal of authority with which to lead? Unfortunately, this frequently isn't true.

My friend and fellow West Point graduate Colonel Jack Gillette commanded fighter squadrons for years. As a squadron commander, Jack had a lot of authority. He commanded his fighter pilots, and they did what he told them to do.

One day Jack was assigned to duties as a program manager managing the development and testing of the F-111 airplane. This was back in 1969 when this airplane was new. There are two versions of the F-111. One is the straight fighter version. Two squadrons of these aircraft participated in the strike against Libya a few years ago. The other version, designated the FB-111 was a bomber that is used by Strategic Air Command.

Jack had two groups of pilots flying airplanes for his program, one for each version. Each group reported to a different Air Force colonel. But neither of these colonels reported to Jack! The fighter colonel reported to a general in Tactical Air Command. The bomber colonel reported to a general in Strategic Air Command. Jack, in Air Force Systems Command, was in charge of the F-111 test program. The only people he commanded were one secretary and one sergeant.

As Jack told me, "It's a real test of my leadership. When I want a test flight made, I can't order a single pilot into the air. I have to persuade either the fighter or bomber commander to do that for me."

Jack was successful because he is a superb leader. His dilemma, however, was not unique. It is familiar to tens of thousands of program managers in government and industry across the country. These leaders have authority over their programs, but limited or no authority over the people who work on them.

When Does Persuasion Work?

Persuasion can also work well when leading others who have similar or more power in the situation than you have. This is especially true when you have no other way of rewarding or punishing someone.

Let's say you are the leader of a group of volunteers, or must get other leaders at your level to follow you. Maybe you must induce a group of your superiors to follow your lead. In all of these situations, consider persuasion as an influence strategy for getting others to follow your lead.

What means can you use to implement the persuasion strategy? One way is to convince through logic. Simply give the person you want to lead good reasons why he or she should do what you want.

This works in more situations than you might think. Not too long ago a social scientist looked at the motivation one person used in getting others to do things. He found that frequently the logic for persuading does not need to be perfect. The person doing the persuading only had to give a reason for wanting the action performed.

During one study, this scientist discovered that many people would allow someone to cut ahead of them in a line to make copies on a office copier only if a reason were given. Did the reason have to be compelling? Hardly. The person had only to say: "Can I go ahead of you because I have to make copies?"

I know this sounds crazy, but apparently the key was simply to give a reason. Just giving the reason was itself sufficiently persuasive. What the reason was wasn't important.

Now I don't recommend your giving just any reason when you use persuasion. But giving some reason is always important. It may be particularly important when leading Americans.

What Baron Von Steuben Discovered
about Leading Americans

Baron Von Steuben came from Germany to help General Washington during our War of Independence. His contributions in helping Washington to create a disciplined army were significant. His influence can even be found in the way the army does certain things to this day.

When General Von Steuben first encountered American troops however, he was absolutely amazed. "Back home," he wrote a friend, "I need only say 'do this,' and the soldier does it. Here in America, I must also give a good reason for my order. Only then does the soldier do what I say."

Everyone wants to know why you want them to take a certain action. This is true whether you have authority over them or not. My personal feeling is that this is something that you owe to those you would like to follow you. And giving reasons why the order is given has an important fringe benefit. When the situation changes and you aren't available to give new instructions, this person knows what you are trying to do. He or she can alter their actions based on why you wanted the actions taken in the first place. You will find that you and your organization will be much more successful at reaching goals than would otherwise be the case.

Another Way of Using Persuasion to Lead

Another way of utilizing the persuasion strategy is to emphasize your personal need or the worthiness of your cause. Remember the young bond salesmen who became the vice-president in Chapter 1? You can bet that in addition to speaking about competing with other company units, he also talked about the advantages of having savings bonds. He might have also said something about his personal need as a new employee with the responsibility for heading up the bond campaign.

Have you ever been approached by a young door-to-door salesperson who emphasized his or her personal need? It may have been a young man or woman working his or her way through college by selling magazines. It could have been a boy scout or girl scout competing for an award. It might have been a high school or college student gaining experience in real business. All of these are examples of persuasion by emphasizing personal need. They are used because they work.

One of the most valiant actions in English history was due partially to the use of leadership through the influence strategy of persuasion.

On January 22, 1879, the British forces at Rorke's Drift in Natal, Africa, were attacked by more than 4,000 Zulu warriors. These warriors were incredibly brave. During an earlier battle against several thousand British soldiers, they were completely victorious.

The British force was not large. There were thirty-six men in the hospital with a surgeon, chaplain, and one orderly. There were also eighty-four infantrymen and a company of Natal Kaffirs. By the time the battle started, including the sick, the English had only 140 effective fighters.

There were two lieutenants. Lieutenant John Chard was senior by less than a year over Lieutenant Gonville Bromhead. Lieutenant Bromhead actually had more total service. He had twelve years to Chard's eleven. In addition, Lieutenant Chard was an engineering officer and held no command at Rorke's Drift. Lieutenant Bromhead commanded the infantry company.

Bromhead wanted to use his infantrymen independently. Using the persuasion strategy backed up by good reasons, Chard convinced Bromhead to accept his leadership. These reasons were his seniority in rank, that a fort-defense represented an engineering problem and not an infantry problem, and the urgency for one overall commander.

The battle lasted from the late afternoon until the following morning. The Zulus attacked repeatedly without regard to loss. When the battle ended about seven o'clock in the morning, Chard had only eighty men left. But the fort held, and the Zulus withdrew.

The highest award the British have for heroism is the Victoria Cross. It is at the same level for heroism in combat as the Congressional Medal of Honor in the United States. Eleven Victoria Crosses were awarded as a result of this battle. This is more than ever given for a single engagement, and it was won by almost 10 percent of the soldiers who participated in the battle.

Both Chard and Bromhead received the medal, and both were promoted to Brevet Major.

The influence strategy of persuasion can be pretty important![3]

Using Negotiation as an Influence Strategy

Another important influence strategy is negotiation. Negotiation means that you influence by conferring with others to arrive at a settlement which you (and those you lead) find acceptable. It may involve compromise or exchanging something that the other person wants done for what you want done.

Negotiation may be required under certain circumstances. Does what you want done offer little or no perceived benefit to the person or persons that you want to influence? Do you and those you want to lead have about equal power? Can both sides help or hurt each other almost equally? If these are your conditions, you may need to use the negotiation influence strategy.

Let's look at an example. In a university, the addition of new courses must be voted upon by all departments. New courses may be perceived as attracting students from one department to another. Thus there may be no reason for a department to vote for another department's proposal for a new course.

If you want to lead in getting the university to offer a new course, part of your leadership may involve using a negotiation strategy. How can you do this? You could offer to support another department's proposal for a new course. Or you could offer something else that the other department wants in exchange for its support for your proposal.

How George Washington Used the Negotiation Strategy in War Leadership

Is a negotiation influence strategy ever a part of military leadership? Most certainly. It is necessary and used frequently when different types of forces such as army, navy, air forces, and marines are employed together. It is also used when forces of more than one nation are employed together in a combined operations.

George Washington gave us a successful demonstration of the negotiation strategy in a battle that was important in winning American independence.

During the War of Independence, our French allies had a contingent of the French Army with General Washington under General Jean Rochambeau.

By the summer of 1781, the two allies realized that the British strength was divided into two strongholds: New York and Chesapeake Bay. These British forces were stronger than the allied American-French force. But together, the combined allied force was stronger than either British force if faced separately. If the two British forces could be cut off from each other they could be defeated individually.

The French had a strong fleet in the area of the West Indies under the command of Admiral Francois de Grasse. However, the hurricane season started in late summer and grew progressively worse in the fall. De Grasse did not want to get involved in a campaign in the north for fear of having his fleet destroyed by storms.

Washington's original plans called for defeating the British in the Chesapeake Bay area, and then moving south for an attack on Charleston or the British base at Wilmington. He got De Grasse to support him by the negotiating strategy.

Washington wrote Admiral de Grasse: "If you sail north and can keep command of the sea during my operations against the Chesapeake Bay force, you can return to the West Indies immediately thereafter."

In other words, Washington let de Grasse off the hook for supporting other allied operations that year in return for his immediate services against the British Chesapeake Bay forces.

De Grasse answered Washington that his fleet would be available until mid-October.

On August 30, De Grasse's fleet arrived off of Yorktown, Pennsylvania. He also brought reinforcements and siege artillery. More importantly, he took command of the sea and isolated the British forces under Lord Cornwallis. Six weeks later, Cornwallis surrendered.

The Battle of Yorktown is known as the decisive battle of the War of Independence. Based on the battle's results, the British opened peace negotiations the following spring.

How General Eisenhower Used the Negotiation Strategy

Another military leader who was a master at leading through negotiation was General, later President, Dwight D. Eisenhower. During World War II, he commanded more than three million allied troops. Among the commanders of these allied armies were very strong personalities such as Patton and the English Field Marshall Montgomery. These men were experienced combat leaders. Commanding foreign troops is always tricky, because their senior most commanders usually have direct communication with the leaders of their governments.

For example, during World War I, General Pershing, commander of the American Expeditionary Force (AEF), was subordinate to the French Field Marshall Foch. Foch ordered Pershing to split up the American units as replacements for allied combat losses. Pershing refused and insisted that the AEF would fight as a unit, or wouldn't fight. President Wilson backed him up.

That meant that though Eisenhower might have the title of Supreme Allied Commander, he had to be very careful of how he commanded.

To complicate his problem, Eisenhower himself had never been in combat. During World War I, he was such a terrific trainer and organizer that he was put to work as a 23-year-old lieutenant-colonel getting tank troops ready for battle in France. Though he tried numerous times to get himself shipped to France, he spent the entire war stateside.

Yet Eisenhower lead this incredibly large number of different soldiers in the largest invasion ever attempted. He was successful largely through using the negotiation strategy. He influenced by getting support of the leaders of the second largest country contingent, the English. And he influenced the English by giving them the senior command positions under him.

If you want proof, you need only look at where Eisenhower's senior commanders came from.

Eisenhower's deputy commander was RAF Chief Marshall Sir Arthur Tedder. The overall commander of allied ground forces was British General Sir Bernard L. Montgomery. The invasion armada was under British Admiral Sir Betram Ramsay. Finally, British and American tactical air forces were commanded by RAF Marshall Sir Trafford Leigh-Mallory. There can be no clearer evidence of Eisenhower's use of the negotiation strategy.

How to Use the Involvement Influence Strategy

If you can get others involved in what you want done, they will adopt your goal as theirs and become committed to its attainment.

That's one of the secrets of one of the major element of Japanese management. The Japanese call this technique ringi. What Japanese leaders do is to take extraordinary pains to insure that leaders and workers at all levels make an input into a proposed action. Until everyone has an opportunity to study and comment on the proposal, the action isn't taken.

Executives from other countries who do business with the Japanese sometimes get extremely frustrated with ringi. Decisions which take days in the United States may take months in Japan.

However, once the decision is made the entire Japanese organization is totally involved and committed to a successful outcome. The Japanese then implement their decision amazingly quickly and effectively.

In comparison, decisions made in American organizations are sometimes made quickly, but are very difficult to implement. The reason is that many members of the American organization are neither involved nor committed to the action or goal.

Ownership of Ideas and Leadership

Why is involvement so important? One dimension is ownership. We work and fight much harder for things that are our own. As a corollary to this, ideas from someone else do not become our own instantaneously.

Dr. Chester Karrass has devoted much of his life to the science of negotiation and has written several well respected books on the subject. He cautions us to allow enough time when introducing new ideas. "Introducing ideas," he says, "is like introducing new friends. It takes time to know and understand people before someone else's friends become our friends as well. Therefore, when you introduce new ideas to someone else, you must give them sufficient time to get to know them before you can expect agreement."

So involving people succeeds as an influence strategy because it gives those whose support you need a sense of ownership. But we must allow sufficient time for this ownership to take place.

Three Important Subsets
of the Involvement Strategy

In her research, Pamela Cuming found that there are three subsets to using the involvement strategy to influence. These are:[4]

- Sharing
- Enabling
- Cooperating

All three have to do with building on the ideas of others. You do this in such a way that your ideas, contacts, and other resources, and those from people you lead are pooled and exchanged. Something greater results that neither you nor those that follow you could have come up with individually.

The Importance of Sharing Information

Please note that sharing information with others is exactly opposite of the way that many leaders mistakingly try to lead. These leaders horde information and refuse to share it with anyone. They seem to think that if they keep information to themselves, they will look smarter than those they want to follow them.

How wrong they are! When you are the leader, it is those who follow you that make you look smart, or not as the case may be.

If those who follow you make errors because they are missing information that you could have given them, you will ultimately suffer far more than they. This is because it is you who is responsible for everything your organization does or fails to do, and no one else.

I once saw a leader go to extraordinary lengths in using the involvement strategy and in sharing information with someone he led.

This leader was the manager of research and development for a company developing and manufacturing ear protectors for the hearing protection of industrial workers subjected to high levels of noise. His name was Bob.

A new government specification required increased levels of protection at both high and low levels of sound for one type of ear protector. This company had been unable to provide it despite an extensive research and development program. Thousands of dollars had been spent in trying all sorts of materials to no avail. They all failed the acoustical test required by the government in either the high or low levels of sound at one or more frequencies.

I happened to be in Bob's office when the latest results from tests on several materials were brought in. Once again, all failed the test. However, as Bob pointed out to me, one material passed at all of the frequencies at the lower level. Another passed on all frequencies at the higher level. The obvious conclusion was to try the two in combination.

George, the project engineer, had been working so long and hard that he had only looked at the failed results, and not put two and two together.

Bob asked George to come to his office. I thought that Bob would point out the obvious and might even criticize George for failing to do a full analysis. At the very least, I fully expected Bob to take the credit for the discovery of what ultimately was found to be the solution to the problem.

Boy was I surprised.

Bob started by saying that he had been going over the results and was impressed at the thoroughness with which George was conducting the testing.

He looked at the results and said, "George, you know this is exactly how Thomas Edison would solve a problem. He would keep testing things and analyzing the results until he found the solution. I know you will eventually find the solution this way as well.

"Sometimes an analysis and comparison is as valuable as the test itself. I know you haven't had an opportunity to analyze this data yet, so here it is. Let me know if you come up with anything."

George left with the data. I stared at Bob in amazement. He only laughed. I asked him why he hadn't shown George what he had shown me.

"Look, George is a good man. He's been working hard on this project for months. He wanted to get the results to me, even bad results, as soon as he could. So he didn't spend much time analyzing the data. Had he done this, he would have seen the same thing I showed you. Now he has the opportunity. It is only fair that George discover the solution. Besides, how much good to me would George be in the future on this project if his boss got the credit for solving the problem?"

Fifteen minutes later George called Bob enthusiastically with the same solution that Bob had showed me. Further, he had an idea for modifying the materials as they were used in combination to make them perform even better. As I said, the solution Bob had originally shown me was found to work. But George got the credit and continued to do good work as an engineer for Bob. He did such good work that both he and Bob were promoted. Bob eventually became president of that company. Are you surprised? I'm not either.

How to Use the Direction Influence Strategy Correctly

There are two situations where simply giving orders with no discussion is your best strategy. The first is where there is little time for using the other strategies. What you need done needs to be done now, with no time for discussion. In combat, the leader must frequently be authoritarian and rely heavily on direction for influence. There is no time for dilly-dallying when lives are at stake or when a slight delay can cause a major defeat.

The second situation when you should use direction is when the action you want done may be good for the organization, but is less desirable for the individual. You need a report typed by tomorrow morning, but your secretary has social plans for tonight. While you can try to use the other influence strategies first, eventually it may come down to using direction.

Unfortunately, the direction strategy is much overused. One reason is probably the popular image of the leader from the movies. The leader runs around barking orders, and everyone else simply falls into line. That's not leadership, that's Hollywood!

In the military they say that the higher in rank an officer goes, the less you see him (or her, nowadays) bark orders.

General A. A. Vandegrift was a marine's marine. He commanded at the Battle of Guadalcanal, one of the most famous Marine victories of World War II. It was there that he issued the order to his command which ended with the stirring words: "God favors the bold and strong of heart."

Did General Vandegrift run around day in and day out barking orders? Here's what they said about him. You can judge for yourself.

"He is so polite and so soft spoken that he is continually disappointing the people whom he meets. They find him lacking in the fire-eating traits they like to expect of all marines, and they find it difficult to believe that such a mild-mannered man could really have led and won the bloody fight."[5]

Another reason that the direction influence strategy is overused is that once you begin using it routinely, it becomes habit. It's so easy. You don't have to think about those you lead at all. You simply issue an order.

A retired four-star general once jokingly said that his biggest shock after retirement was that he got in the backseat of his car and gave an order, but the car didn't move because he no longer had a driver.

Unfortunately, routinely using direction can have unwanted results. You may no longer get input from those you lead. "Fine," say your followers, "If that so and so wants us to do this and everything gets screwed up, its not our fault." Soon, your organization is brought to a standstill. Yet everyone goes about following your orders to the letter. And that's just the trouble.

Another reason that you don't want to use the direction strategy under all conditions across the board is that, even if it works, it might not be in your own best interests.

I knew a young lieutenant once who used the direction strategy so frequently that he used it not only in leading his subordinates, but also his colleagues and superiors. The amazing thing was that for awhile he was successful. He was so bold in giving his direction, and frequently right, that everyone just did what he wanted. That is, until he was relieved of command and discharged for receiving a bad officer's effectiveness report. What was his offense? The report didn't use these words, but it boiled down to one fact. He used what is a perfectly good influence strategy under inappropriate conditions. You can lead your boss and your associates, but rarely by giving orders.

Never make a habit of using direction as an influence strategy under all conditions. But when time is short, or the action you want done can hurt the person that must perform this action, the direction influence strategy may be required.

The four basic influence strategies that you can start using now are:

1. *Persuasion.* Use this strategy when your authority is limited and others have similar or more power in the situation than you. In this case, give others a reason to follow you and emphasize your personal need and the worthiness of your goals or objectives.

2. *Negotiation.* Use this strategy when the perceived benefits by those you want to lead are limited and their power is about equal to yours. Offer something explicitly in exchange for their followship.

3. *Involvement.* This is a very powerful motivator; therefore, use it as a strategy whenever you can. All you need to do is to give those you lead some ownership in your ideas, goals, and objectives.

4. *Direction.* Use this strategy when time is too limited for the other strategies. Remember that you must have more power than those you lead to use direction effectively.

Understanding the four basic influence strategies will go a long way toward enabling high performance as a leader in a variety of situations. However, there are occasions when somewhat different leadership influence strategies are required. These are the three manipulation influence strategies that you will learn in the next chapter. You will also learn when and when not to use them.

ENDNOTES

[1]Adolf Von Schell, *Battlefield Leadership* (Quantico, VA: The Marine Corps Association, 1982), p. 15.

[2]Pamela C. Cuming, *The Power Handbook* (Boston: CBI Publishing Company, Inc., 1981), p. ix.

[3]Byron Farwell, Queen Victoria's Little Wars (New York: Harper and Row, 1973).

[4]Pamela C. Cumings, *op. cit.*, p. 100.

[5]*The Armed Forces Officer* (Washington, DC: U.S. Government Printing Office, 1950), p. 83.

Chapter 6

THE THREE MANIPULATION INFLUENCE STRATEGIES

The three influence strategies you will learn in this chapter are not straightforward regarding either your aims or your means. This does not necessarily make them wrong when they benefit those you lead. It does mean that you must use them infrequently and that they must be for the benefit of others, not yourself. Manipulation strategies are more risky than the other four strategies because:

- they can cause negative feelings
- they can cause a future lack of credibility
- if the action they cause turns out to be wrong, you may not be forgiven

The risk is acceptable when:

- they are used for the primary benefit of your mission, task, organization, and those you lead . . . not yourself
- the situations are dangerous or critical
- the four basic influence strategies either can't be used, won't work, or are less effective

The Three Manipulation Influence Strategies

The three manipulation influence strategies are:

- Seduction
- Redirection
- Repudiation

Let's look at each of them in turn.

Using the Seduction Influence Strategy

A seduction influence strategy is used when your authority is informal, rather than formal, and you don't want those you lead to know where they are being led.

Do you have children? By now you know when they begin to be particularly nice, offer to do extra work, or tell you how well you look, watch out! You are about to be lead by the seduction influence strategy.

Your children have no formal power in the family. As parents, the formal power is yours, but you are being led by the informal power of charm.

Do you know where you are being led? You may not now, but you soon will. Chances are your son wants to borrow the car, or your daughter wants to go out on a date in the middle of the week. Or, it may be something else.

If our children did this all the time, it wouldn't work. Still, it's amazing how often we do allow them to lead us this way even though we know what's happening. And so, Johnny gets to use the car and Sarah gets to go out Wednesday night even though we intended to encourage her to stay home and study.

The Day That George Washington Used the Seduction Strategy and Saved the Country

After the Revolutionary War, the Continental Army had not yet disbanded and Congress was being a bit slow in authorizing back pay. The righting of various other wrongs had been frequently promised by the Continental Congress, but never done. The officer corps of the army banded together and formed an association called the Cincinnati Society through which they intended to revolt and force Congress to do their bidding.

The leaders of the Cincinnati Society knew that George Washington would never go along with seizing power from the civilian authority, no matter how just the cause. But Washington was no longer their official commander, and so had no formal power. They didn't invite him to their meeting; however, he learned of it and asked to be allowed to speak to them.

Washington spoke to these officers for more than an hour. Remember, these weren't mercenaries or shirkers. Among them were many of the heroes of the revolution. Men like Alexander Hamilton, John Knox, and "Light Horse" Harry Lee all listened to Washington. He talked about why they had fought, what would happen should they rebel, and what Congress was trying to do. It was to no avail. Too many times before they had received promises from Congress only to see these promises broken. These officers were determined to take the law into their own hands!

Finally, Washington reached into his pocket and pulled out his pair of spectacles. No one had ever seen Washington with spectacles.

As he slowly put the glasses to his face, he said his final words to the Cincinnati Society. "Gentlemen, I have grown old in your service and now I am growing blind."

There wasn't a dry eye anywhere. As Washington turned to go, there were already calls for the vote against rebellion. And of course, the rebellion never took place.

What his officers didn't know was that George Washington had worn spectacles for years. Because of vanity he had never worn them in public. Even his closest aides didn't know that he wore glasses. Washington judged that the loss of his vanity was a worthwhile price to pay for an America free from military dictatorship. He used the seduction influence strategy to gain such enormous sympathy that the Cincinnati Society could not go against his wishes.

When and How to Use the Influence Strategy of Redirection

The leader using redirection doesn't want to reveal the real reason for the action he wants done. He wants to redirect those he leads because if he does not do this it will have a negative impact of one kind or another.

Let's say there are two organizations whose offices are located right next to each other. The members of these organizations are constantly bickering. The fact that they are located so close to one another allows increased opportunity for hostile contact. So, the organizations are physically separated by having their offices moved away from one another. Does the memo announcing their move state that they are being relocated due to their bickering? Of course not. The stated reason is probably "efficiency," or "better space utilization."

Redirection is also used when firing senior managers. Senior executives are rarely officially fired. Rather, they are given new assignments. We say that they are "kicked upstairs."

This is a perfectly legitimate strategy with many advantages. We preserve the feelings of the fired executive to the maximum degree that we can. We show others that people are important to us. We just don't throw people away like old shoes when they fail. Finally, an individual unsuitable for one job can do a superior job at a different time and at a different place.

Remember Colonel Kyes, the Wing Commander who rebuilt the Bomb Wing in the Air Force back in Chapter 1? Colonel Kyes fired many people. Later, some were deservedly promoted to important jobs by none other than Colonel Kyes himself.

Eisenhower's Use of the Redirection Strategy

In February 1943, Eisenhower met his first defeat in Tunisia when Rommel unexpectantly attacked and rolled back his line at the Battle of Kasserine Pass. After the battle, Eisenhower concluded that he had to replace one of his senior commanders, Major General Fredendall. Fredendall was sent back to the states and replaced by someone who everyone came to know–a fifty-six year-old major general by the name of George S. Patton.

What happened to Major General Fredendall? He was eventually given a training organization in the states. He did such a good job, that he was eventually promoted to Lieutenant General.

How "Sam" Grant Used the Redirection Strategy

Ulysses S. "Sam" Grant was the man that Lincoln finally found to beat Robert E. Lee. To beat Lee, Grant also used the strategy of redirection to influence his men.

At his first battle against Lee at the head of the Army of the Potomac, Lee won the day and Union forces retreated. As they retreated out of the wilderness, the Union columns got only as far as the Chancellorsville House crossroad. There they encountered a squat, bearded general smoking a cigar and sitting on horseback. As the head of each regiment came abreast of him, he took out his cigar and pointed to the right fork. That's where they went. They thought they were retreating, but the right fork led right back into battle against Lee's flank.[1]

Redirection can also be used to get the minds of those you lead focused on other things.

One scene in the television series "Baa Baa Black Sheep" showed this clearly. One of Pappy Boyington's squadron members came to him with a problem. Thinking about his first combat on the coming day, this pilot was afraid to fight!

Instead of consoling him, Boyington said only, "I think I have something that's going to help you."

With that, Boyington hauled off and decked him. Responding out of instinct, the pilot got up and punched Boyington. Before it could go further, Boyington pointed out that in the heat of battle he would forget his fears.

How to Use the Influence Strategy of Repudiation

In using the repudiation strategy, the leader gets someone to do something by disclaiming his or her own ability or power to do it.

An analyst goes to his supervisor and asks for help in doing some problems. "Gee, I'd like to help," his supervisor says, "but I haven't worked this type of analysis in quite a long time. How would you approach them? Why don't you start out. Maybe I'll remember a little."

So the analyst begins to work the analysis. Whenever he gets stuck, his leader gets him going again. The supervisor used the repudiation strategy to get the analyst to learn to do the job and to actually do the job at the same time.

The repudiation strategy can also be used by subordinates to lead their bosses, or by managers to lead other managers. "Boss, I have a problem and I wonder how you would handle it?" The boss is flattered to be asked. Most bosses are more than willing to help out.

Peter Drucker's Example

Peter Drucker once pointed out that the empathy built with the boss in this way is probably more beneficial to the organization than the subordinate's always going off by himself and working out the solution without a consultation. That's not to say that a leader should never work out his own problems or that he must consult his boss about everything. But most executives probably do not consult with their bosses as much as they should.

In one company Drucker observed two vice-presidents of different operating divisions. While equally competent and with similar backgrounds, each had an entirely different method of operating.

One consulted with the president of the company about his problems fairly often. He used the repudiation influence strategy to lead his boss. The other vice-president did everything on his own. He kept the president informed about his decisions, but never talked a problem over with him unless the president requested it.

Both got equally good results. After three years, the president announced his retirement. Which vice-president do you think he picked to replace him? According to Drucker, it was the one that consulted with him frequently.

The Repudiation Strategy and Boss Sponsorship

I believe that the reason the repudiation strategy with your boss can lead to support is that your boss becomes your sponsor. Research of top managers both in and out of the military has discovered that no leader reaches the higher levels of the executive suite without a "sponsor." A sponsor is someone who has found a subordinate whom he or she thinks has special ability. The sponsor keeps an eye on the protege and in various ways helps his or her career along. Sponsorship, which is also known as "mentoring," has almost become structured in some companies.

General George C. Marshall carried sponsorship to an artform. He kept his own list of up and coming young officers and their qualifications over a period of thirty years. When World War II came, General Marshall was Chief of Staff of the Army. His knowledge and sponsorship of the young officers he had noticed years earlier led to the elevation and promotion of men like Eisenhower, Bradley, and Mark Clark.

However, if you are going to use the repudiation influence strategy with your boss, you must be extremely careful. You can use repudiation to lead your boss, but do not expect an automatic sponsorship. There is the question of time and individual preferences. Your boss may prefer that you work your problems out on your own. Finally, if you force the relationship, you're going to get in trouble with your boss as well as other managers at your level.

Nobody likes what has been called variously "the teacher's pet," "a brown nose," or more kindly, "a fair-haired boy."

Many managers use the repudiation strategy to lead other managers at their levels. Instead of competing in an area in which the other manager excels, the good leader disclaims his own ability and thereby gets his colleague to do what he wants: "Joe, you're the best softball coach the company team ever had. I'm going to recommend that you be named the coach this year again."

When to Use One Influence Strategy Over Another

One of the most valuable lessons you can learn about using the four basic and three manipulation influence strategies is that there is a time and place for all of them. If you have one strategy that you rely on almost all the time you are almost certain to get into trouble. Stop and think if one of the other strategies might not be more appropriate and might lead to better results.

Your selection of a particular strategy will depend on:

- the individual personality of the person or persons you are leading
- the mood of the person or persons
- your own current frame of mind
- your goals or objectives
- the relative power between you and those you lead
- the importance of time in the action you want taken
- the type of commitment you require for completing your desired action
- rules, laws, or authority you may have in the situation

The seven strategies can also be used in combination, or one after the other. It is worthwhile to reread how General MacArthur insured that one of his new battalions was successful in its attack its first time in combat. See just how many different influence strategies General MacArthur used in combination.

Certain influence strategies tend to work better than others as time passes. A new company or organization is formed. The leader emphasizes attracting qualified people. This requires persuasion strategies. As his organization grows, team building and the exchange of ideas becomes more important. Involvement strategies should be used. Now the organizational units are formed and the biggest question is how the work should be divided up. This requires negotiation. Now the company is into production. Tasks are more routine, but are time-critical. This calls for more direction. Throughout, seduction, redirection, and repudiation may be used.

The Three Manipulation Strategies—When or When Not to Use Them

Remember that manipulation strategies are risky. They should only be used for the benefit of your people or your organization, never yourself. They are most suitable for situations where the four basic influence strategies either can't be used, won't work, or are less effective. This is especially true in dangerous or critical situations.

- Use seduction when your authority is informal, rather than formal, and you don't want those you lead to know where they are being led.
- Use redirection when you don't want to reveal the real reason for the action you want done.
- Use repudiation when it is important to disclaim your own power or ability to get something done.

One strategy is not the best under all conditions. Any of the these strategies may be the best depending on a variety of factors. So in every case the effective leader must consider all of his or her options and all factors in deciding which strategy or combination of strategies to use.

Now you are ready to strengthen your leadership self-confidence for increasingly more difficult leadership tasks. To do this, turn to Chapter 7.

ENDNOTE

[1]*The Armed Forces Officer* (Washington, DC: U.S. Government Printing Office, 1950), p. 83.

Chapter 7

HOW TO DEVELOP YOUR SELF-CONFIDENCE AS A LEADER

There is an old story told about the Texas Rangers. It happened around the turn of the century. One of the wild gangs that roamed the old West took over a small Texas town. They shot up the bar, threatened the citizens, and drove the sheriff out of town. In desperation the town's mayor telegraphed the governor, pleading that he send a detachment of Texas Rangers to right the situation. The Governor agreed that the problem called for the famous Rangers. The Governor promised that a detachment would be on the next day's train.

The mayor himself met the train on which the Rangers were to arrive. Unbelievably, only one Ranger got off the train.

"Where are the rest of the Rangers?" asked the mayor.

"There aren't any," was the answer.

"How can one Ranger handle the gang?" asked the mayor indignantly.

"Well, there's only one gang ain't there?" replied the Ranger.

This story may not be 100 percent true, but it is based on fact. Less than 100 Rangers protected the entire State of Texas. And no Ranger felt himself outnumbered, though he might be working alone. The Ranger would look the situation over, and do what had to be done. He would lead posses, motivate and organize disheartened citizens, and guide lawmen. The situation was almost always dangerous. Yet the Ranger routinely led and directed others in life and death situations. From such facts came legends like the story

I've told you, or the fictional hero "The Lone Ranger" that you may have heard of.

What Is the Secret that Empowers Leaders?

How is it possible that leaders take charge and assume responsibilities for lives, jobs, and billion dollar companies? How is it possible that leaders can take responsibility for the future of nations, if not mankind itself? How is it possible that leaders sometimes lead thousands, or even millions of men and women in accomplishing something? Yet they may do all of these things seemingly without blinking an eye. Where do they get such tremendous self-confidence?

Self-Confidence Comes from
Knowing That You Can Succeed

An old Air Force training manual on leadership says "No man can have self-confidence if not convinced in his own mind that he is qualified to perform the job he is assigned."[1]

It's a fact. If you know that you can succeed at something, then you will have self-confidence that you can do it. The truth is, it is impossible not to. So the problem is: How can you know you will succeed before you actually try something?

General Curtis LeMay built the Strategic Air Command into the mightiest military force ever forged. Later he became Air Force Chief of Staff. Before World War II, he was a thirty-year-old captain and a B-17 navigator. Officially he led only himself. Five years later, he was a major general leading thousands. He was not only responsible for their lives and well-being, but for the success of missions crucial to the outcome of the war.

Early in the war LeMay was sent to Europe as a Colonel and Group commander. The bombing results before LeMay arrived were terrible. This was because of heavy concentrations of anti-aircraft artillery efforts by the Germans.

"You can't fly straight and level for more than fifteen seconds," the "old timers" told LeMay. "If you do, you'll get shot down."

Now a bomber needed to be a stable platform to deliver its bombs accurately. The bombardier had to identify his aiming point and accurately determine the winds that would affect the bombs after release. The plane had to avoid evasive action for a lot longer than fifteen seconds; otherwise, the bombardier had no real chance to hit his target.

LeMay looked at his losses and at the results. Because results were so poor, his planes had to return to the same targets again and again.

He soon gave new orders. "Every plane will fly straight and level for at least ten minutes prior to 'bombs away.'" The experts gave him warning that his entire force could be destroyed. LeMay listened to the experts, but remained convinced that he was right.

His crews bombed after a ten minute straight and level run from an initial point. The bombs hit accurately on the target. Although losses per mission increased, losses for each target destroyed declined significantly. Eventually, LeMay was promoted to Brigadier General.

Two years later, LeMay was sent to the Pacific Theater as a Major General to head B-29 operations against Japan.

The B-29 was a remarkable airplane. It was designed as a "Superfortress" with guns bristling from all quadrants. Its four powerful engines were designed to take the plane at an altitude far above the effective range of the antiaircraft guns. The B-29 had a sophisticated pressurization and oxygen system, and in many other ways was optimized for use as a high altitude bomber.

The B-29 was an expensive airplane for those days. So much so, that General Hap Arnold, Commanding General of the Army Air Forces, told LeMay that the B-29 should be treated differently than other less expensive aircraft. Arnold felt that the loss of a single B-29 in combat or by accident should require more than a routine investigation. He told LeMay that he should consider treating the loss of each B-29 in the same way that the Navy treated the loss of a capital ship like a carrier or battleship.

LeMay began his operations. Once again, bombing results were poor. The culprit now wasn't antiaircraft artillery. The B-29 flew well above that. The problem was wind shear. The winds at the altitudes that the B-29 flew were vastly different from the winds at the lower altitudes above the target. Also, the winds acted on the bombs for a much longer time than bombs dropped at lower release altitudes. So the bombardiers lost control of where their bombs hit. They might hit anywhere, and they definitely weren't hitting their targets.

LeMay looked at the situation and listened to the recommendations of the crews and his staff. Then he made his decision. He ordered all oxygen and pressurization equipment removed. He ordered the guns removed. Since there were no guns, the gunners wouldn't need to go either. Removing all of this weight allowed more bombs to be carried. Then he proposed that his B-29s bomb—not at 29,000, but at 7,000 feet.

Again, experts told LeMay that he was wrong. They informed him that he would lose his entire fleet of aircraft. They also told LeMay that General Arnold would relieve him of command for wasting the lives of his crews and for not using the expensive high-altitude and defensive capabilities that had been built into the airplane.

LeMay ordered his crews to bomb at 7,000 feet. The results were devastating—to the Japanese. LeMay got far greater results for lower losses than any air campaign in the war.

How did General LeMay summon up the courage and self-confidence to make these decisions and take these great risks? Where did such self-confidence come from in an individual who only a few years earlier commanded a single group, and only a few years before that commanded nothing?

Without a doubt, LeMay believed he would succeed before he gave the orders to carry out his instructions in both instances. What gave him the idea he would succeed?

How to Know That You Will Succeed Ahead of Time

There is an old saying that nothing succeeds like success. This means that success breeds success, or that successful people tend to become more successful. In other words, if you have been successful in the past, you have a better chance of being successful in the future.

But how can you become successful until you have already been successful? It's like the chicken and the egg. You can't have a chicken until you have an egg, but you also can't have an egg until you have a chicken.

Fortunately, you can have a number of small successes before a big success. And small successes counts just as much as a big success as far as your belief system is concerned. Therefore, if you can win little victories in being successful at something, your psyche will believe that you can accomplish even greater things in the same area.

Many leaders are trained this way. They acquire their self-confidence and self-respect by leading successively larger organizations with greater responsibilities. At every step, their belief that they can be successful grows. As we have seen, the belief that you will be successful leads to the self-confidence necessary to do the job.

You Don't Need to Be an Expert in Everything

It used to be thought that leaders grow into their jobs because of the technical experience and product knowledge that they acquire at each step. However, in this age of technical specialization, it is virtually impossible to be an expert in everything all of those you lead do. This means that the technical knowledge is of far less importance than how you train your belief system.

As a Reserve Air Force Officer, I worked for a very successful General Officer who commanded important research and development organizations. Yet her background was not in engineering, but in personnel.

A good example from industry would be John Sculley. He left a very successful career as a senior executive with Pepsi-Cola to become the President of Apple Computer. Other than the fact that they are both products, the differences between computers and soft drinks are far greater than their similarities. Yet Sculley was successful as a leader in both positions.

You May Not Have the Opportunity
to Grow into a Leader

Unfortunately many individuals may not have the opportunity to be trained by leading successfully larger organizations. Some individuals are so valuable to their bosses that they can't be spared for jobs where they would lead organizations. Others are overlooked until later in their careers. Then they had better be ready, whether they led smaller organizations or not.

Want an example? Look at General of the Army Dwight David Eisenhower. By the time he was elected President, Eisenhower already had a lot of experience in leading men and women in very large organizations. However, as we will see, he lacked some experience that many would consider important before he became a general.

In 1940, General Eisenhower was a Lieutenant Colonel. Despite many requests to be sent overseas during World War I, he spent the entire war training troops in the United States. He never saw combat. Between wars he did valuable work in a variety of staff jobs. He was so valuable in fact, that he despaired of ever being assigned to command troops again.

With the buildup just prior to the war, he was assigned to the General Staff as a Colonel in 1941, reporting to the Army Chief of Staff, General George C. Marshall. Marshall promoted him successively to Brigadier General and Major General. A year later, after completing plans for joint allied operations in Europe, Marshall sent him to London as the Commanding General, European Theater of Operations. The year after that he commanded the allied invasion of North Africa, and eventually became the Supreme Commander for the allied invasion of Europe. Finally, he wore five stars as General of the Army.

Please note that after years of staff positions, and never having been in combat, Eisenhower eventually commanded and led more than three million fighting troops of many different nations. Then later, as President, he went on to lead the most powerful country on earth.

This Man's First Supervisory Responsibility Was for an Entire Company

Peter Drucker, the famed author, professor, and management consultant, once used a similar case study from his personal experience in a graduate course that I was privileged to attend at Claremont Graduate School in the mid-1970s.

Like Eisenhower, Drucker was a company executive with legal training and had spent his entire career on staff. Then one day, as a senior staff vice-president, the Board of Directors had elected him President of the corporation. This was his first real line job, and like Eisenhower, he was leading thousands.

Four Ways to Build Your Self-Confidence and Your Leadership Skills

How Do Leaders Get the Self-Confidence They Need to Lead? How do leaders like this new company president, General Eisenhower, and hundreds of others acquire the belief in success necessary for the self-confidence to do the job?

I'm going to give you four ways to build your self-confidence and develop your leadership skills. These methods have been used by President Eisenhower and thousands of others. If you adopt them, you will develop your self-confidence as a leader by numerous smaller successes. Every time you practice them, your belief system in your own success will be strengthened. You will become a powerful leader. Like General Eisenhower, you will be ready to assume major leadership responsibilities because you will have the self-confidence to do it.

After returning to troop duty after more than eighteen years on various staff assignments, General Eisenhower wrote: "I have in the few short months I have been allowed to serve with troops, completely reassured myself that I am capable of handling command jobs."[2]

Eisenhower was a Lieutenant Colonel at the time, but he already had the self-confidence in his own leadership for higher levels of command.

The four ways are:

- Become an uncrowned leader
- Be an unselfish teacher and helper of others
- Develop expertise
- Use positive mental imagery

Take Advantage of the Fact That You Don't Need to Be a Manager to Be a Leader

The first way to develop self-confidence while you develop your leadership skills is to become an uncrowned leader. There are hundreds of opportunities for you to become a leader if you want to. I promise you that if you stop to look you will find at least one opportunity, and probably even more, every day. The truth is, people around you are positively crying for you to help them by seizing the opportunity to lead.

Remember, you don't have to be a manager to be a leader, and as I pointed out in an earlier chapter, the two are not even the same. Being a manager has to do with doing things right. Being a leader has to do with doing the right things. You absolutely do not need to have an official position as a paid manager to be a leader.

Can You Become an Uncrowned Leader?

What is an uncrowned leader? An uncrowned leader just means that you will seek out and accept leadership jobs outside of your normal responsibilities. You may or may not get paid in dollars for your accomplishments as an uncrowned leader. But the self-confidence you will get from doing uncrowned leadership jobs and the skills you will acquire will more than make up for it.

How to Become an Uncrowned Leader

The first rule for becoming a successful uncrowned leader is to accept responsibility cheerfully on the job. Even more than accepting leadership responsibility, you must seek it every chance that you get.

Remember the young manager in Chapter 1 that was promoted because he did such a great job in leading a bond drive? Well the bond drive falls into the uncrowned leader category. You can do the same thing as that young up and comer. I don't mean that you necessarily must lead a bond drive. There are lots of other opportunities.

Is there is a special report that needs to be written? Is the boss looking for someone to organize or coach your company's sports program? Does your office need a new computer? Who's going to handle the job of selecting and buying it? Do you have office parties or weekend get-togethers? Entertainment committee chairmen are in leadership positions also. Every organizing opportunity is another chance to be an uncrowned leader.

The more you do this, the easier it gets. And, the more others look to you as their leader, the more self-confident you will become in your ability to lead.

How to Find Uncrowned Leadership Jobs

Your uncrowned leadership jobs don't need to be just at work. There are cases every day where there are immediate problems that need to be solved and need a leader to help others to solve them.

Look around and you will see that everyone is looking at everyone else to lead. No one seems to know what to do. Do you know what to do? Are you at least willing to try? If so, you will be instantly and automatically promoted to uncrowned leader.

The strange thing is that in most cases you will discover that it is not that no one knows what to do, it is that no one wants to do the work or to take the responsibility for doing whatever needs to be done. Under these circumstances, you will be amazed at just how ready others are to follow your lead.

You Don't Need to Fight for Uncrowned Leadership

Now please don't misunderstand me here. There are also situations that you find yourself in where it seems that everyone wants to lead. In some of these cases, people want to lead so badly that they will actually fight each other to do so.

You may or not be able to help out here as the group's leader. Whether you can or not, you are unlikely to be asked. When you find yourself in this kind of situation, my advice to you is to sit back and stay out of the fight. If the situation is so critical that some act needs to be done, do it yourself. Help the group as best you can, but don't compete for leadership. No matter how terrific a leader you are, you can't and won't lead in every situation you find yourself in. But that's not important. There are plenty of uncrowned leadership opportunities around.

As Al Garsys, a good friend and a Marine Corps Colonel says, "I can lead, and I can follow. An important aspect of leadership is knowing when to do which."

More Uncrowned Leadership Opportunities

Since there are far more uncrowned leadership opportunities than there are leaders, you will find opportunities to lead everywhere. You will find many opportunities where you live. There are neighborhood committees such as the "neighborhood watch" to help your local police guard against crime, to beautify the neighborhood, to get out the vote, and many others. There are numerous committees that require leadership positions if you live in an apartment or condominium.

You will find other opportunities to lead in your church or synagogue, professional organizations, trade associations, political organizations, boy and girl scouts, and many others.

Believe me when I tell you that there are many more uncrowned leadership jobs than there are leaders to fill them. Look for unpopular jobs that no one wants to do. Volunteer to do them and have fun doing them. Your self-confidence will soar as you become more and more successful as a leader.

Be an Unselfish Teacher and a Helper of Others

In the first chapter I explained that we succeed in life only to the extent that we help others succeed in their lives. That's true whether you are a leader of men in combat, in the office or boardroom, or even an author of a book on leadership.

If I am successful in helping you to reach your goals in life as a leader, you will make me successful in my goals as an author as well. That's how life works.

So to become a successful leader there is something you must do. You must give up some of your time, some of your resources, and some of your self so that others can succeed.

In doing so, you will develop the self-confidence and success in uncrowned leader jobs without which you cannot move on to bigger leadership jobs in the future.

An Officer and a Gentleman Is First and Foremost a Leader

Did you see the movie *An Officer and a Gentleman*? In it, the hero does very poorly in naval officer training. He fights and is disrespectful to his superiors. Contrary to regulations, he shines the shoes of his classmates for money. The only thing he does right is the obstacle course. On the obstacle course, he is really good. He is so good, that it appears that he will set a training record when the class is required to run it officially.

Then he gets in serious trouble when his best friend commits suicide and he challenges the noncommissioned officer in charge of his training. He is certain to be eliminated from officer training. However, while his dismissal is pending, his class runs the obstacle course for the record.

One of his classmates is a woman that always has trouble climbing over one of the obstacles. As the hero runs on to set his record, she becomes stuck on this obstacle. It's the hero's moment of decision. What will he do? The only thing he had done well in the entire training program was the obstacle course. Perhaps if he sets a record, he will not be dismissed.

The hero stops and goes back to help his classmate though he knows this will cost him the record he hoped to set.

It is this one act of helping someone else that causes the powers that be to let him graduate and become "an officer and a gentleman."

This is the exact thing that I am talking about. If you want to build your self-confidence so that you will be a great leader, teach and help others, even at cost to yourself.

Teachers and Leaders in the U.S. Army

Back in 1932, an article on the U.S. Army appeared in the German journal *Militar Wochen Blatt*. The article was written by Captain Adolf Von Schell of the German Army. He had attended and lectured at the U.S. Army's Infantry School at Fort Benning, Georgia.

Captain Von Schell stated that the chief role of the American regular officer was, "teacher and counselor." He went on to raise an important question. "But if the American officer is primarily a teacher with his principle training in schools, does sufficient time and opportunity remain to develop him as a leader?"

Von Schell concluded that while everything was done to train American officers as both teachers and leaders, that the training of both at the same time was not possible.[3]

Less than ten years later, men like Marshall, MacArthur, Eisenhower, Patton, and Arnold proved Von Schell wrong.

Many Teachers Became Great Military Leaders

Perhaps it is no accident that many teachers in civilian life have made good military leaders. "Stonewall" Jackson, the hero of the Confederacy, was a professor at Virginia Military Institute before the Civil War.

In the same war, Colonel Joshua Chamberlain, commander of the 20th Maine, saved the Union line on Little Round Top on the second day of the Battle of Gettysburg. Chamberlain had been a professor of rhetoric at Bowdoin College. He finished the war as a Major General.

Robert E. Lee had been Superintendent at West Point before the Civil War. Lee turned down offers of considerable sums of money to become the president of a small college.

Of our World War II leaders, almost every single one had taught somewhere, whether it was at West Point or Annapolis, a civilian institution, the Infantry School, or one of the many military colleges.

Please don't think my words are too much self-serving when I remind you that your author is also a university professor—and was a navigational and combat flight instructor as well.

Why is experience as teacher of such importance? Because teaching is a more structured way of giving of yourself to help others. In teaching, you will gain additional success and confidence which will help you as a "paid" or official leader.

Why You Should Develop Your Expertise—in Something

Research has demonstrated conclusively that there is an important source of power that will automatically attract others to you and make you their uncrowned leader. That source of power is expertise.

What is expertise? Expertise is in-depth knowledge or skill about some subject. Expertise can be on any subject. It can be about marketing, flying, warfare, management, stock management, recordkeeping, investments, buying a car, getting a loan, bowling, or baseball. Expertise can also be on what to eat, how to jog, or even the best way to mow your lawn. Expertise can be about anything human beings do.

Expertise and Its Ability
to Make You a Leader

Now you must understand one important fact about expertise and its ability to make you a leader. Any expertise will cause people to seek you out as a leader. However, the frequency that people make you a leader because of expertise depends on one factor. That factor is how relevant your expertise is to the people around you.

Let's say you have expertise as a bowler. Many people will seek you out and make you a leader—if you are in the company of other bowlers. If you want to be an uncrowned leader in a group that has few bowlers, don't depend on bowling expertise. Few will be interested!

To maximize your leadership opportunities through expertise, just be sure that your expertise is relevant to the group. In other words, your expertise matches the needs of the people around you.

If you have expert knowledge about how to do something important to the group, there just isn't any question but that you'll be sought out as a leader. You will have increased opportunities to lead, and you will gain self-confidence as you do this.

How a Young Lieutenant Became a Major
in Three Years . . . in Peacetime!

During my first flying tour of duty in the Air Force, I saw a young lieutenant join our wing who became an expert navigator. Three years later, this young man became a major—all through his special expertise in navigation.

During World War II, young men barely out of high school became colonels through their expertise at various tasks. Many in their early twenties advanced rapidly through their ability to fly fighter aircraft and shoot down enemy planes. Robert S. Mc-Namara became President John F Kennedy's Secretary of Defense. During World War II, he advanced from the rank of captain to lieutenant colonel in four months because of his expertise in mathematical techniques of analysis.

How George S. Patton
Became a General

Certainly one factor that led to Patton's promotion to general just before World War II was his expertise with tanks. During World War I, George Patton had been a full colonel at the age of only twenty-nine. He had led America's first tank unit in combat. However, because of budgetary cutbacks, the Army had to reduce its number of tanks. Patton went back to the horse cavalry and returned to the rank of first lieutenant. By 1940, he had worked his way back up to colonel. Then the Army needed someone with tank expertise. Patton was one of the few senior officers that had that expertise. The Army quickly made him a general.

How Expertise Helped Others
on Their Way to the Top

Many "fast burners" in industry got to the top rapidly for the same reason. These include Steven Jobs, who founded Apple; Lee Iacocca of Chrysler; William McGowan, chairman of MCI; Frederick Smith, founder and chairman of Federal Express; and many others. They all shared a common attribute—they had expertise in a topic that was of some importance to others.

How Ray Kroc Used Expertise to
Build McDonalds

Did you think that Ray Kroc, who founded McDonalds, became a multimillionaire simply because he went into the hamburger business? Not on your life! Many companies made hamburgers before McDonalds got into the business, and while McDonalds was growing every year, the other companies were still losing money.

No, Ray Kroc didn't invent the hamburger. But Ray brought a new dimension to the hamburger business because he had developed a special expertise. He not only knew how to make good hamburgers, Kroc knew how to have others make identical high-quality hamburgers at low cost. He used a combination of unique instruction, quality control of methods and franchisees, and techniques such as special measuring cups. Through his methods, even a high school student could make quality hamburgers. It made no difference whether the McDonalds was located in the north, south, east, or west. The hamburgers were always the same, and they were always good.

If you want people to acknowledge you, or even to seek you out as their unofficial leader, all you need to do is develop a needed expertise.

Revealed: The Secret About Acquiring Expertise

Now listen. Here's what I find interesting about acquiring expertise. Not only is it interesting, it seems to be a big secret because not too many people seem to know it. You can become an expert in just about anything in only five years or less. There is only one requirement. You must put forth the effort.

Proof That You Can Become
an Expert in Anything in Five Years

Want proof? Jobs and Wozniak were college drop-outs when they founded Apple Computers and became multimillionaires. But they had been working on building computers even in high school. The time it took them to become computer experts? About five years.

Dr. Kenneth Cooper has probably made more contributions to health by preventing heart attacks than any man alive. It was Ken Cooper who conducted the research and developed the concept of aerobic training when he was a flight surgeon in the Air Force. His numerous books, lectures, and aerobic centers in Dallas, Texas, have helped millions on the way to good health and prevented millions more from unnecessary, premature, death. His efforts got the whole country jogging, walking, cycling, swimming, and doing other healthy activities.

When Dr. Cooper first presented his research and proposed that his aerobic training be adopted throughout the Air Force, it did not gain immediate acceptance. Some older, far more experienced flight surgeons didn't believe it would work. They couldn't believe that anyone could acquire so much expertise in such a short period of time. You guessed it. When Ken Cooper first developed his theories, he had been working on aerobics for heart exercise for only five years!

Do This Research to Convince Yourself

If you further doubt what I say about how long it takes to become an expert, I challenge you to do a little research. I want you to go to newspapers, magazines, and books, and look up the careers of young men and women who are supersuccessful. I recommend that you look for young people because otherwise you may be tempted to fool yourself and count the total years of experience, rather than only the years spent acquiring a particular expertise.

For example, Colonel Harland Sanders was well past sixty when he began to market his secret family recipe which eventually led to the multibillion-dollar Kentucky Fried Chicken franchise.

You could say that he spent his entire life acquiring expertise in the fried chicken business. However, you would be wrong. He didn't begin to learn anything about fried chicken until he was sixty-two.

I suggest that you look at the careers of supersuccessful people who are young not because older people can't become super-successful. They can. Harland Sanders and Ray Kroc are just two examples from thousands. However, if you look at younger successes, there will be no doubt regarding how long it took to acquire the needed expertise.

Now, I'm not saying that you will always find success in five years. Sometimes success takes much longer. Yet we're not talking about success here. We're talking about expertise. If you want to be an expert at flying, karate, dancing, marketing, or business, you can do it. You can acquire the expertise you want and it will only take you five years or less.

Expertise Is Not Automatic

But don't forget. Acquiring the expertise is not automatic. You must put forth the effort required to do it. If you do, like Jobs, Wozniak, Kenneth Cooper, and so many of hundreds of others, you will have the expertise, and people will seek you out as their leader.

Developing Self-Confidence
Through Positive Mental Imagery

One of the most important exercises you can do to develop your self-confidence as a leader is practice positive mental imagery. The effects of positive (and negative) imagery can best be illustrated if I give you an example you can try for yourself.

Imagine a two by four plank constructed of hard wood, twenty feet long placed on the ground. If I put a $50 bill at one end and told you all you had to do was to walk across the plank to keep it, you would have no trouble. You would stride confidently across and pick up the $50 bill.

What if I raised the height of the plank to fifteen feet off the ground? You would probably still get to the $50, but it would be a lot more difficult. You would be much more careful where and how you stepped. Your stride would be much slower and more deliberate. What is the difference between the two situations? The distance to the $50 bill hasn't changed. The width and construction of the board hasn't changed in any way. Nor has the location of the $50 bill relative to your starting position. Only the height has changed, and that shouldn't really make any difference. Or should it?

Now let's raise the height of that plank to 300 feet between two skyscrapers. Are you still ready to go for the fifty? Or would you insist on at least a thousand dollars or more to walk across the twenty-foot plank? Even then you might decide not to try it. If you did, I bet you would be mighty careful. Yet nothing has changed except the height. The plank, distance, width, and location of the money haven't changed a whit.

The real difference, of course, is the difference in mental image which the difference in height creates. When the plank is on the floor, our mental image focuses on the fifty dollars. However, as the height increases, we focus not on the fifty dollars, but on falling and the consequences of the fall.

Positive or Negative Mental Imagery
Can Have Crucial Effects

Karl Wallenda was probably the greatest tightrope walker that ever lived. He walked across great distances, high in the air, and he did so without a net. Further, Karl Wallenda didn't stop his breathtaking walks as he grew older. He did the same fabulous stunts in his seventies that he had done in his twenties.

Then in 1978, while performing a tightrope walk between two buildings in San Juan, Puerto Rico, he fell to his death.

Several weeks later, his wife was interviewed on television regarding Wallenda's last walk. "It was very strange," she said. "For months prior to his performance, he thought about nothing else. But for the first time, he didn't see himself succeeding. He saw himself falling."

Wallenda's wife went on to say that he even checked the installation and construction of the wire himself. "This," she said, "was something Karl had never done previously."

There seems little doubt that Karl Wallenda's negative mental imagery contributed to his falling.

Positive Images Can Significantly Improve Your Self-Confidence

Just as negative images can hurt your self-confidence as a leader, positive images can help your self-confidence considerably.

One of the leading researchers in the area of imagery is Dr. Charles Garfield. Dr. Garfield is a unique individual. He has not one, but two doctorates: in mathematics and psychology. I first read of Dr. Garfield's work in the pages of the *Wall Street Journal* in 1981. The article spoke about Dr. Garfield's research regarding what he called a kind of "mental rehearsal." Garfield found that more effective executives frequently practiced mental rehearsal. Less effective executives did not.

In his book, *Peak Performers*, Garfield describes how his theories were confirmed by Soviet bloc performance experts in Milan, Italy, in 1979.

Garfield is an amateur weight lifter. At the period in question, he hadn't worked out in several months. When he had, his best lift had been 280 pounds, although he had done more previously when he had worked out regularly.

The Soviets asked him what was the absolute maximum he thought he could lift right at that moment. He responded that he might be able to make 300 pounds in an exercise known as the bench press. In this exercise, you are flat on your back. You take a barbell off of two uprights. Next you lower the weight to your chest and then you return the weight to the starting position.

With extreme effort, he just managed to make that amount. As Garfield himself said, "It was difficult—so difficult that I doubt I could have done it without the mounting excitement in the room."

The Soviets then had Garfield lay back and relax. They put him through a series of mental relaxation exercises. Then they asked him to get up slowly and gently. When he did, they added 65 pounds to the 300-pound weight. Under normal circumstances, it would have been impossible for him to lift this weight.

He began to have negative images. Before they established themselves in his mind, the Soviets began a new mental exercise.

"Firmly, thoroughly, they talked me through a series of mental preparations. In my mind's eye I saw myself approaching the bench. I visualized myself lying down. I visualized myself, with total confidence, lifting the 365 pounds."

Much to Garfield's surprise, he not only lifted the 365-pound weight, but he was also astounded to discover it was easier to lift than the lighter weight had been earlier.[4]

You Can Use Mental Rehearsal
to Build Your Self-Confidence

I have used mental rehearsal techniques for many years. I can guarantee that not only will you find them effective, but that they are easy and painless with no aftereffects.

The secret is to first relax as much as you can, then to give yourself positive images. What I do is this. I lay back and get as relaxed as I can. Then I start with my toes and tell myself that my toes are becoming numb. I repeat this suggestion to myself several times.

From my toes, I go to my feet, legs, torso, and so on. In every case, I repeat the suggestion that the particular part of the body I am focusing on is becoming completely relaxed and numb.

When I am totally relaxed, I go to work on my positive imagery. Let's say that the leadership situation that I want to build self-confidence in has to do with a meeting I am going to run.

In my mind, I will picture everything about that meeting in detail. I will see the table, the lighting and the decorations. I will see the sights, hear the sounds, smell the smells, and feel every sensation. I will see every individual who is participating in that meeting. I will rehearse every item on the agenda. In my mental imagery I will rehearse not only what I will say, but the responses from those I will lead as well. Naturally, in my mental rehearsal, everything will go the way I want it to go. In fact, I will make sure that all of my mental image rehearsals go perfectly.

After I complete the rehearsal once, I repeat the entire rehearsal again. I do it several times at a sitting. If the situation is particularly important, I may repeat the entire mental imagery process a couple times a day for several days.

Does it work? Amazingly, I have rarely failed when I used this imagery technique. It is true that reality does not always follow my preplanned script. Sometimes the changes are significant. But the results gained by seeing a favorable outcome over and over again has a dramatic effect. I never lack self-confidence in any leadership situation which I have mentally rehearsed.

Four Action Steps to Building Leadership Self-Confidence

You can develop your leadership self-confidence by taking four action steps. All have to do with one basic fact. Your self-confidence will increase as you accomplish leadership tasks successfully. So do smaller and easier tasks first. Take on all that you can and then progress to more difficult tasks. You will find them to be much easier than you thought.

Here are the action steps to build leadership self-confidence:

1. Become an uncrowned leader by seeking out situations and volunteering to be a leader whenever you can.

2. Be an unselfish teacher and helper of others. Others will come to you for leadership.

3. Develop your expertise. Expertise is a source of leadership power.

4. Use positive mental imagery. Simulations in the mind are rehearsals for success. They are interpreted by the mind as real experiences. So they will boost your leadership self-confidence just like the actual experience.

ENDNOTES

[1] *AFM 35-15 Air Force Leadership* (Washington, DC: Department of the Air Force, 1948), p. 30.

[2] Edgar F. Puryear, Jr., *Nineteen Stars: A Study in Military Character and Leadership*, 2nd ed. (Novato, CA: Presidio Press, 1981), p. 155.

[3] Adolf Von Schell, *Battle Leadership* (Columbus, GA: The Benning Herald, 1933), pp. 92–94.

[4] Charles Garfield, *Peak Performers* (New York: Avon Books, 1986), pp. 72–73.

Chapter 8

HOW TO BUILD YOUR ORGANIZATION LIKE A WINNING FOOTBALL TEAM

In my seminars on leadership, I always ask this question. Can you think of any organization which has all of these attributes?

- The workers work very hard physically, including weekends, with little complaint.
- The workers receive no money and little material compensation for their services.
- The work is dangerous and workers are frequently injured on the job.
- The work is strictly voluntary.
- The workers usually have very high morale.
- The organization always has more workers than can be employed.
- The workers are highly motivated to achieve the organization's goals.

Do you think that there's no such organization on the face of the earth? That such an organization can't exist? That such an organization is only in someone's dream?

Before you come to such a conclusion, consider a high school football team. It has all of the above qualities. Do you say that a successful high school football star can go on to make megabucks

as a professional player? Well, that's true; however, the chances of
that happening considering the numbers of high school players
versus the numbers of pro players is very slim indeed. Very few
perform "work" on a football team for that reason.

What You Can Learn from a Girls' Soccer Team

I have selected football as my example, but you can find similar
or even more amazing results in other sports. In Scarsdale, New
York, Arthur Resnick coaches a girls' soccer team.

In a four-year period, Coach Resnick's team won seventy-five
consecutive matches. Of course it won the regional title every year.

I know what you're thinking. This is one of those schools that
trains professional athletes. Every student is a "jock." The male
teams have achieved even more dramatic results.

All of these statements are 100 percent wrong. This is not a
particularly athletic school. Other teams at the same school, both
male and female, have only a mediocre record.

Coach Resnick's techniques have been studied by others because of his incredible success. Stories have appeared about him
and his team in magazines and newspapers including *Business
Week, Wall Street Journal* and *Boardroom Reports.*

Why are business and management readers so interested in
what the coach of a girl's team did? Because they realize that if
they can understand what Coach Resnick used to build his girl's
soccer team, they can use the same techniques to build their own
organizations.

Is There a Correlation
Between Leadership and Athletics?

There is some correlation between leadership on the athletic
field and leadership in other things in life. After the First World
War, the authorities at West Point decided to review the records
of former cadets. They wanted to know whether there was anything in the records of cadets who later became general officers
that could have predicted their success. Academically, there were
no predictors. There were generals who graduated first in their
classes, such as MacArthur; however, there were also generals
who graduated last in their classes, such as Custer. There were also
generals who had been athletes, and generals who had not. But it
was a fact that a West Point graduate had a better chance of

becoming a general if he had been an athlete while a cadet. As a result of this research, athletics became required for all cadets.

General Douglas MacArthur's View

General Douglas MacArthur's view is known to every West Point cadet. It is blazoned in stone on the main athletic building at West Point: "On the fields of friendly strife are sown the seeds, that on other fields, on other days, will bear the fruits of victory."

Military leadership attempts to replicate athletic leadership on the playing field. Its many successes are demonstrated by elite military units as well as the sometimes incredible accomplishments and victories in combat against great odds by winning military "teams."

What an organization you can have if you lead your organization or group like a winning football team! What accomplishments are possible! What victories can be won!

In this chapter, we're going to learn to apply the techniques used by every winning coach as well as every winning battlefield commander to build an unbeatable team.

What Every Winning Athletic Team Has

If we want to build an organization like a winning athletic team, we must first examine winning teams to see what makes them successful. Successful athletic teams have these characteristics:

- *Cohesion.* Cohesion means sticking together. It means that members put the interests of the group over their own interests.
- *Teamwork.* Teamwork means working together so as to maximize the strengths of individual group members and minimize their weaknesses.
- *High Morale.* Morale is an inner feeling of well-being that is independent of external factors.
- *Esprit de Corps.* Esprit de corps is a French word which has to do with the morale of the organization as a unit.

In this chapter, we'll look only at cohesion and teamwork. In Chapter 9, we'll examine the characteristics of high morale and esprit de corps.

What Is Cohesion?

Cohesion is known in the military as a combat force multiplier. This means that the mere existence of strong cohesion in a unit can multiply the effectiveness of this unit in combat. Through strong cohesion, a smaller and weaker military force can overcome one that is larger and stronger.

Many units that fought in Vietnam lacked cohesion. This was because of the Army's policy of rotating individual men stateside as they completed one year of combat duty. As a result there was little unit stability as replacements constantly arrived and veterans departed. The Army could have maintained the cohesion of these units by rotating the entire unit and replacing it with a new one. This policy contributed to a decrease in unit motivation, disciplinary, and combat performance.[1]

Cohesive Organizations Outperform Others

Cohesive organizations outperform organizations that lack cohesion again and again. Not too long ago, a researcher studied cohesion in some detail.

Lieutenant Colonel Jon W. Blades, an Army officer at the National Defense University in Washington, D.C., investigated this aspect of cohesion. Blades discovered that a noticeable increase in cohesion was accompanied by significantly better average performance scores in each of four major training areas that he measured.

According to Blades, cohesion had this effect because good working relationships among the members of the group made more efficient use of group assets. Such assets might include the ability of the group's members, available time, and assigned equipment.

Blades also found that a positive increase in group performance was seen in basic training among training platoons which had high cohesiveness. These highly cohesive platoons almost always performed better in such soldierly skills as rifle marksmanship, physical fitness, drill and ceremonies, and individual soldier skill tests, than did platoons with low cohesiveness.

Why was this? Because in the more cohesive platoons, the more talented soldiers voluntarily spent their free time teaching and coaching those that were less talented. From this, Blades concluded that if members had high ability and high motivation, the more cohesion a group would be and the better the group performance would be.[2]

If you have ever seen a mediocre athletic team that has played together for a while beat a newly formed all-star team, this may be the reason.

An Air Force Fighter Pilot Demonstrates Cohesion

During the 1958 Lebanon crisis, an Air Force fighter pilot who had very limited training on his type of aircraft was ordered to fly from his base in South Carolina to Adana, Turkey.

He ran into bad weather. He considered aborting the flight and turning back. Instead, he pressed on. His inexperience led to difficulty in locating his tanker aircraft. Over the middle of the Atlantic Ocean with only four minutes of fuel left, he was desperate. He thought about ejecting from his aircraft and leaving it to crash. Then just in time he found his aerial tanker and took on the necessary fuel.

Some hours later, he landed at Adana. When he was asked about his experience, he said, "In my worst moment, I suddenly realized that staying with my gang meant more than anything in the world."[3]

Other studies of men in combat confirm the feelings of this young airman. Army historian Brigadier General S.L.A. Marshall, who conducted more than 400 interviews with American infantrymen immediately after combat in both the European and Pacific theaters of war, concluded that the main motivation for a soldier to fight is a sense of psychological unity with other members of his immediate combat unit. Said General Marshall: "I hold it to be one of the simplest truths of war that the thing which enables an infantry soldier to keep going with his weapons is the near presence or the presumed presence of a comrade."[4]

Sure patriotism, religion, and ideology are strong motivators. However, "staying with the gang," a good description of cohesion, is even stronger. That's true in battle, and its true in your organization as well.

How to Develop Strong Group Cohesion

If you want to develop strong cohesion in your organization, you must develop pride in membership in your organization. To feel pride, your group must feel that they are in the best organization of its type, anywhere. That is, if your organization is a production crew making automobile parts, each member must feel that he or she is in the best production crew making automobile parts in the world. If your group does management consulting, then every member must feel that he or she is in the world's best management consulting group. The same principle applies regardless of what kind of business you are in. Every one of your group must feel that he or she is in the best organization of its kind.

How to Convince Your Group
That They Are the Best

Now, if you are going to convince your group that they are the best, they are actually going to have to *be* the best in some way. This is not as difficult as it appears. The key is to focus on some element that is important to the group and to concentrate on being the best at that.

The obvious things are things that can be measured: sales, units produced, awards received, and so forth. However, measurables need not be involved, as long as group members have a valid reason for believing that they are the best.

One squadron that I flew with prided themselves at being the best at night attack. Another squadron on the same base felt that they were the best at low-level flying. I have seen members of organizations that felt that their organizations were the best of their type for all sorts of reasons. These included:

- the hardest workers
- the organization that got the toughest assignments
- the organization that worked the longest hours
- the fastest
- the most courteous
- the most thorough
- the most creative
- the most productive

I have also been in a group that thought itself the best of its type because it was the most fun-loving! This was a section of fifteen officers and government executives at the Industrial College of the Armed Forces selected by accident as being most representative by background. This group played together, went to school together, and had such a good time while learning that their seminar number became famous throughout the college.

As the group's leader, it's up to you to develop this "we're the best" attitude. Here are some more hints as to how to do this.

You can do this right at the start, when you first become associated with your group. Assign tasks that you know those in the group can perform well. As their skill and pride of accomplishment increases, select tasks that are progressively more difficult.

Of course, every time a task is completed successfully, make certain that the individuals completing them receive the recognition they deserve. And make certain that your entire organization learns of every victory.

Recognition comes in variety of forms. Official letters of commendation are one way. However, even short, handwritten notes and verbal praise are appreciated.

I'll have more to say about recognition in a later chapter.

You can and should encourage organizational mottos, names, symbols, and slogans. West Point does this extensively. Every cadet company has a motto—and there are thirty-six cadet companies. First-year cadets are required to greet their upperclass companymates with the company motto. Army units do much the same thing.

Establishing a Group's Worth

Finally, you can improve group cohesion by establishing the worth of the organization and its values.[5] The more good things that you can find and can say about your organization, the better. Everyone likes to be associated with winners and winning organizations. No one wants to be in an organization that is thought of as losing. So if you can establish your group as a winner based on its past, you are well on your way toward a strong, cohesive unit.

What you can do is this. Investigate and find good things in the history of your organization. What are your organization's traditions? What has your organization accomplished in the past that you can promote? The more you can find to promote, the better.

Note that I keep mentioning promotion. Once you ferret out this information about your organization, you've got to use it. You want everyone in your organization to know what a terrific outfit they are associated with. Publicize this information in newsletters. Post it on bulletin boards, read the information at staff meetings. Use every technique you can to promote your organization as the best around. Get people excited about their membership in the group. Make them feel that they are better than anyone else—the best.

Now I must give you one cautionary note here. Some leaders think that they can promote their organization best by tearing down the reputation of the parent organization. This is a mistake. It will only backfire. Not only will your superiors eventually come down on you, but you will destroy the very cohesion you are trying to build. Once again, no one wants to be associated with a losing organization, even if it is the parent organization to their own. So don't do it. Even when things go wrong because of actions of the parent organization—but your own organization has done its job—build support for both organizations; don't assist one at the expense of the other.

On the other hand, if the members of your organization feel that they are in the best organization of its type, you will build a bonding force that is stronger than super glue. It is a cohesion that cannot be broken, and it will pay dividends.

How to Develop Winning Teamwork

If you have watched successful athletic teams performing, you were probably amazed at just how easy they made their accomplishments look. So integrated was the performance, that instead of seeing the individual members acting, you saw the team as a single entity in motion.

You may even have been seduced into thinking, "Boy, that's not so hard. I can do that." So if you participate in the same sport, or coach young people, you may have tried the same play of teamwork you saw performed by experts. Only then did you realize just how difficult it was for a group to do what you saw the well-coordinated team perform.

This type of teamwork occurs in situations other than athletic events. In the military, such performances happen daily on aircraft, ships, tanks, in missile and artillery command centers, and field training exercises. The performances are amazing. Not only does every team member seem to know exactly what to do, but also how to modify his or her individual performance to fit in with changes in the environment and minor changes in the performances of other group members. The bottom line is that through teamwork, the overall performance is greater than the sum of the performances of all of the individual team members.

Peter Drucker's Phenomenon

Peter Drucker found the same phenomenon in a well-run hospital. Doctors, nurses, X-ray technicians, pharmacologists, pathologists, and other health-care practitioners all worked together to accomplish a single objective. Frequently he saw several working on the same patient under emergency conditions. Seconds counted. Even a minor slip could prove fatal. Yet, with a minimum amount of conscious command or control by any one individual, this medical team worked together toward a common end and followed a common plan of action under the overall direction of a doctor. The similarity to what you saw on the athletic field would be striking.[6]

Teamwork in all activities is crucial. Years ago, the Air Force did a study of their bomber crews in the Strategic Air Command. Individual performance improves with increased flying experience as measured by number of flight hours. These researchers wanted to know how performance was effected by increased flying experience on a specific aircraft. They thought that similar to flying experience in general, more experience on a particular airplane would cause performance to improve. It did. However, the time a crew spent flying together was a far more accurate predictor of improved performance than individual flying experience.

What an Israeli Army Study Showed

An interesting study by the Israeli Army again confirmed the importance of teamwork. The Israelis analyzed the combat performance of their soldiers in the Golan Heights in Northern Israel. Using peer evaluations, the Israelis found that the quality of combat performance was highly related to teamwork in fighting together and much less on individual fighting qualities, or even commitment to goals of the war effort.[7]

Coach Frank Leahy's Reflection

Famed Notre Dame football Coach Frank Leahy was an officer in the U.S. Navy during World War II. He watched hundreds of football games, the majority of which he won. He also witnessed the battle for Iwo Jima. After reflecting, he said: "The burning desire to emerge the victor we see in our contact sports is the identical spirit that gave the U.S. Marines victory at Iwo Jima."[8]

How Our Pilots Survived Imprisonment
in North Vietnam

How can you develop teamwork in your organization? One very important thing you must do to develop teamwork is to focus on a common purpose. This should be the overall objective or contribution that you are trying to make.

Our pilots who were shot down and made prisoners during the Vietnam War endured unspeakable hardships, starvation, and torture. At the same time, their captors made them brutally aware of the war's controversy back in the states. Their captors flaunted the fact that at least some Americans thought of them as criminals. Yet they held together, maintaining their faith in their God and their country. They did this because they focused on a common purpose. This was to survive their imprisonment without betraying their country. Despite everything, they succeeded.

It is instructive to know that these beaten, weakened men exercised teamwork in prison even in the face of hardship and death. Forbidden to communicate in any way, they developed the ability to communicate by tapping on adjacent cell walls. In this way, they passed on news, the orders of the senior-ranking American prisoner, comforted each other, and even prayed together.

As new prisoners arrived, they were taught the code as well. In this way, these Americans maintained themselves and practiced a highly developed teamwork. Yet this teamwork was developed at great risk and under the constant surveillance of the enemy. It was developed even though in some cases weeks, months, or even years went by without these men even being able to see one another.

Without focusing on a common objective, little can be achieved. In the Korean War, Americans were also held as prisoners under inhumane conditions, hundreds of whom died during their imprisonment. Medical testimony after the war indicated that many of these deaths were unnecessary since these prisoners were neither stricken by disease nor malnourished to the point of death.[9]

What happened was that our men gradually lost their will to live. Experts tell us that their will to live would probably have been maintained had they banded together early to work for a common purpose. Instead, some collaborated with the enemy for better treatment, and others placed themselves above the common good in other ways.

When I was thirteen years old, my father was assigned as a military attorney to defend an American F-51 pilot, who while a prisoner, falsely confessed on film and radio to North Korean charges of germ warfare. I remember him telling my father that he didn't think anyone would believe his confession. Since it was a lie and he wasn't giving away any military secrets, he didn't think he had betrayed his country.

Years later, as a young flyer myself, the Air Force showed us some of the propaganda films made by the North Koreans. Suddenly on the screen, there was my father's client, apologizing for acts that he had never committed.

When we compare this with the actions of our men while prisoners in North Vietnam, there is little doubt that focusing on the common purpose would have resulted in teamwork instead of dreadful error during this adversity.

Another Way to Develop Teamwork

There is another way that you can develop teamwork in your organization—that is, to encourage your organization to participate in sports together outside of work. You should participate yourself. If it is a sport that you are particularly good in, well and good. If not, that's all right too. The important thing is to play these sports with the members of your organization.

These don't need to be contact sports—and maybe they shouldn't be. Try and select a sport that everyone can participate in, male or female, in great shape or not. What sport you select isn't important. Playing together will help your "team" develop the teamwork which will spill over into other areas of your lives—and that's what you are after. To build your organization like a winning football team, take these actions:

- Develop pride in group membership
- Convince your group that they are the best
- Give recognition whenever possible
- Encourage organizational mottos, names, symbols, and slogans
- Establish your group's worth by examining and promoting its history and values

- Focus on the common purpose
- Encourage your organization to participate in activities together outside of work

Now turn to Chapter 9 to look at two very important concepts for building your organization like an athletic team: high morale and esprit de corps.

ENDNOTES

[1] Jon W. Blades, *Rules for Leadership* (Washington, DC: National Defense University, 1986), p. 75.

[2] *Ibid.*, pp. 76—78.

[3] *The Armed Forces Officer* (Washington, DC: Department of Defense, 1975), p. 6.

[4] S.L.A. Marshall, *Men Against Fire: The Problem of Battle Command in Future War* (New York: William Morrow, 1947), p. 42.

[5] Jon W. Blades, *op. cit.*, p. 100.

[6] Peter F. Drucker, *The Effective Executive* (New York: Harper & Row, 1967), pp. 68—69.

[7] John H. Faris, "Leadership and Enlisted Attitudes," in James H. Buck and Lawrence J. Korb, eds. *Military Leadership* (Beverly Hills, CA: Sage Publications, Inc., 1981), p. 148.

[8] *The Armed Forces Officer* (Washington, DC: Armed Forces Information Office, 1975), p. 157.

[9] *Ibid.*, p. 68.

Chapter 9

BUILDING HIGH MORALE AND ESPRIT DE CORPS

Winning athletic teams have two other characteristics that are important. Usually these two qualities go together. They are morale and esprit de corps, and every winning athletic team has them.

Think of high morale as being a feeling of well-being or exaltation of an individual group member. Collectively, there is also a group feeling of well-being or exaltation. That is esprit de corps.

You need both to build a winning team. In this chapter you'll learn how to do exactly that.

How to Develop High Morale

They say that the biggest difference between the American worker and the Japanese worker has nothing to do with Japanese management techniques. Instead, it's simply that the American worker looks forward to the weekend, and the Japanese worker looks forward to the workweek.

What a difference! When your workers have high morale, they too will begin to look forward to the week rather than the weekend. And why not? People with high morale have fun. Naturally, they look forward to having fun and feeling good. That this will happen during the workweek is good for you. That there are five days of fun and feeling good versus only two on the weekend is good for them. So it's a double win.

How can you achieve this? How can you get such high morale that your workers would rather be on the job working than doing other things?

Cut Others In on the Action

If you want your group to have high morale, you must let them in on the action. By this I mean that your workers must share ownership with you in accomplishing any project or task.

Long before "participation management" the army used to say: "tell your men what to do, but don't tell them how to do it." You can see that if a worker decides how to do something himself, he has a share in ownership.

Admiral Ben Moreell headed up the Seabees during World War II. The Seabees were our naval construction engineers that built important navy bases in combat areas under extremely difficult and hazardous conditions. Moreell said that he had a secret formula that enabled him to get results. "We used artisans to do the work for which they had been trained in civil life. They were well led by officers who 'spoke their language.' We made them feel that they were playing an important part in the great adventure. And thus they achieved a high standard of morale."[1]

One of the greatest management experts of all time was a man by the name of Chester Barnard. Barnard learned his management the hard way. He worked himself up from the bottom at AT&T. Then in the late 1930s, he wrote a book, *The Functions of the Executive*, which is still widely read. His conclusions are worth studying.

Said Barnard: "Scarcely a man, I think, who has felt the annihilation of his personality in some organized system, has not also felt that the same system belonged to him because of his own free will he chose to make it so."[2]

When you give your people ownership, they feel much differently toward the task than if you represent yourself as the only one responsible. The difference is between an important team member and an organizational cog. When you award them ownership, they are under the influence of feelings of an entirely different type.

Colonel John S. Moseby, CSA, was a great guerilla leader during the Civil War. The Union troops called him "the gray ghost" because whenever they thought they had him trapped, he disappeared. Thousands of Northern troops attempted to catch him, but they were never successful.

His exploits were legendary. Once raiding far beyond Union lines, he captured almost a hundred horses, as well as a Union general in bed with his mistress. When told, Abraham Lincoln was said to have commented, "Too bad about the horses. I can replace the general a lot easier."

Why was John S. Moseby so successful? He wasn't trained at West Point, and he hadn't been a soldier before the war. He explained it all in his book *War Reminiscences*, published in 1887. "Men who go into a fight under the influence of such feelings are next to invincible, and are generally victors before it begins."[3]

High Morale and Cheerfulness

Another way that you can influence morale is simply by being cheerful. Cheerfulness in and of itself has a very positive effect on morale.

One of General MacArthur's West Point classmates said that even in the early days, MacArthur imparted his self-confidence to others through his cheerfulness.

A classmate of General Eisenhower's, Brigadier General Carl C. Bank, said: "The one outstanding characteristic notable at all times was his cheerfulness, friendliness, and good humor."[4]

It's a fact that many individuals have attributed their success simply to smiling. An official manual on Air Force leadership published after World War II discussed the leadership of five-star General Hap Arnold who had been commander of the Army Air Force during the war. This manual said that General Arnold's ready smile played a significant part in his being promoted to the command of the Army Air Force. According to the manual, "Cheerfulness spells confidence, optimism, fearlessness, and 'I like people,' which everyone recognizes and warms to immediately."[5]

Be Aware of What's Going On . . . Then Act

If you want high morale in your organization, you must constantly monitor what is going on. Keep your eyes and ears open, look for trends, and most importantly get around to visit and talk with people in your organization every day. That way you'll not only know how your people feel, but you'll also be aware of everything that is going on.

If the people in your organization become depressed, you should know about it instantly, and instantly take action to do something about it. Sometimes a simple joke can turn things around. Other times you may need to do more. The important principle is to know what's going on in your organization, and then to take action immediately to influence it. If you do these two things, you will have a major impact on events rather than the other way around.

Princeton is not only a town where a famous university is located. A major battle was fought there during the Revolutionary War.

This battle was a very near thing. George Washington closely observed his men under fire. He saw that it was becoming too much, that they were in danger of panicking. Once a few men fell back, his entire line could break. Instantly he urged his horse between the American and British lines. He rode up and down between the two lines, ignoring British fire. How could his men be fearful with their commander riding up and back right before their eyes? The truth was that they couldn't, and the Continental line held.

In 1942, Major General Ira C. Eaker of the U.S. Army Air Forces planned daylight bombing missions against the Germans. Royal Air Force pilots told him that it wasn't possible, that losses would be too great. The RAF had a lot of credibility. They had been fighting the Germans and bombing them since 1939. Still, the Americans had been working on new techniques for daylight bombing. Eaker was undeterred from his plans for daylight bombing. However, his men were aware of the opinion of the veteran flyers from the RAF. Eaker also knew that this knowledge had caused some of his men to doubt their own abilities. It isn't everyday that a major general pilots a plane in combat, but Eaker went on that first daylight bombing mission himself. His force went on to employ daylight bombing with tremendous effect throughout the war.[6]

Yes, frequently leading by personal example will do the trick—and you don't necessarily have to put yourself in personal danger.

I mentioned Baron Von Steuben in a previous chapter. He was the volunteer who helped George Washington turn an eager, but untrained, mob of men into a real army during the Revolutionary War. Among his many contributions, he developed our first drill regulations. Remember in those days, drill was not just for training. It was used in combat to insure that men fought and maneuvered together on the battlefield. Without drill, only harassment operations were possible.

Said Von Steuben, "I dictated my dispositions in the night; in the day I had them performed."

Of course, just writing down what to do isn't leadership. What could Von Steuben do to have his drill performed? What Von Steuben did was to form a model company which he drilled himself in what he had developed the previous night. Then he drilled his company in front of the officers and soldiers of the Continental army. In this way, he not only showed them exactly what to do, but he demonstrated that what he wanted done would work on the battlefield.

No wonder Von Steuben became, though a relatively young man, the first Inspector General of the Army.[7]

How Long Does It Take to Build High Morale?

You may have heard that it takes months, or even years to build high morale. Let me assure that this is simply untrue. General George S. Patton said that, "In a week's time, I can spur any outfit into a high state of morale."[8]

Once I saw even the great Patton outdone in building a high state of morale in minimum time. It was in a squadron of attack planes during the Vietnam War. This squadron had low morale because of high losses while flying against heavily defended areas along the Ho Chi Minh trail in North Vietnam and Laos.

The squadron commander hadn't helped morale either. This officer, after having not flown in years, had been plucked from his nonflying role and sent to the war. He was the senior ranking lieutenant colonel, so they made him the commander.

This was a mistake. During his years away from flying and operations, he had lost many of his fighting skills. Worse, in combat he became hesitant. Then, he began to avoid flying the tougher combat missions. Finally, he was relieved of command.

The new squadron commander turned the situation around with only two sentences. He said, "I am your new squadron commander. I am going to fly more missions, and more of the tougher missions than anyone else in the squadron."

Esprit de Corps

Have you ever wished that you could be a military leader, rather than the leader of some other kind of organization? After all, all a military leader has to do is give a command and it is carried out, right? Wrong.

When I first entered civilian life, I was hired to head up a research and development organization. The president of the company called me in and said, "Now, Bill, I know that you have led military organizations, but it's not the same thing leading civilians. You can't just give an order, and see it carried out."

I assured my new boss that in most instances military command wasn't that simple. I did, however, promise to go easy at first.

Now it wouldn't be fair to compare an infantry company, or fighter squadron in combat with an organization that does research and development for a living. However, some kind of comparison can be made between research and development organizations in military and civilian life. Do you know what I discovered? I had a lot more power of command in my civilian organization. Here's why. In the military, if an officer performed poorly as a research and development project engineer, the worst I could do is give him a bad assignment and a poor performance report. In civilian life, if someone performed poorly, I had the power to instantly fire him.

Therefore, regardless of what kind of organization you lead, you must reserve your command authority for those instances when it is appropriate to use it. Your aim should be to build a desire in the individuals in your organization so that they want to be led by you. This organizational consensus for your leadership and the high feeling of spirit associated with it is called esprit de corps.

General Harbord, commenting on his lessons learned during World War I, said in *The American Army in France*, "Discipline and morale influence the inarticulate vote that is constantly taken by masses of men when the order comes to move forward—a variant of the crowd psychology that inclines it to follow a leader. But the Army does not move forward until the motion has carried. 'Unanimous consent' only follows cooperation between the individual men in ranks."[9]

In other words, there is a group spirit that you must reach in order to motivate groups of people to do things—even in the military, and despite the effect of orders.

How do you develop esprit de corps? For my money, esprit de corps is built on three things: your personal integrity, mutual confidence, and a focus on contribution rather personal gain.

Thomas E. Cronin, a political scientist and writer, who was also a White House Fellow, observed that integrity, "is perhaps the most central of leadership qualities."[10]

Major General Perry M. Smith tells a story about Babe Zaharias in his book *Taking Charge*. Babe Zaharias was a champion sportswoman in the 1932 Olympics. Later, as a professional golfer, she penalized herself two strokes after the round she was playing was over. The penalty strokes cost her first place in the tournament. Why did she do it? It turns out that she accidentally played the wrong ball. Later a friend asked her why she penalized herself. "After all, Babe," said the friend, "no one saw you. No one would have known the difference." "I would have known," replied the great Babe.[11]

West Point probably has the strictest honor code in the world. It says simply, "A cadet will not lie, cheat, or steal, or tolerate anyone else that does."

The code is simple, but it is strictly enforced—by the cadets themselves. An honor violation means that the cadet is expected to resign. Let's say that a cadet copies an answer from another cadet's paper during a test. Later, although he wasn't observed, he turns himself in to the cadet honor committee for an honor violation. He is now expected to resign from the Corps of Cadets. If someone had observed him copying an answer, he would have reported it to the honor committee. I have seen both happen when I was a cadet.

Once when I was a cadet and home on leave after my first year at West Point, I went out drinking with some friends from high school. I forgot that the minimum age to drink beer was twenty-one, rather than eighteen as it was in some states on the East Coast. As is popular today, my friends all had fake identification cards which indicated that they were twenty-one. Being accustomed to ordering beer at eighteen, I didn't even think about it. When asked for identification, I presented my cadet identification card.

The barmaid looked at it closely. It didn't have my age, but did identify me as a Cadet at the United States Military Academy. The barmaid looked at the card with my picture and then looked at me. "You can't get a beer here unless you're twenty-one. This says that you are a West Point Cadet. I know that if you tell me you are twenty-one it will be the truth. Are you twenty-one?" I had to admit I was not. My friends couldn't believe it. Like Babe Zaharias, they told me that no one would have known that I had lied. I am proud to tell you more than thirty years later that like Babe Zaharias, I answered, "I would have known."

I have seen men live by this code while cadets, and die by the same code later as officers. The code has saved lives in combat, because what a graduate said could be absolutely depended on as the truth.

This code wasn't started by the officials at West Point. It came from the cadets themselves, back in the nineteenth century. At first, the honor committee's activities were secret, because the authorities resented this assumption of power by cadets. However, as time went on, the importance of absolute integrity was recognized for its value on the battlefield and in all human relationships. So the honor activities were legalized.

There have been rare cheating scandals at West Point, where numbers of cadets have intentionally violated the code. You can count the number of times this has happened on one hand.

I wish I could tell you that all graduates continue to live by the honor code after they graduate. Unfortunately, since we are dealing with human beings, this would be inaccurate. I can tell you that the ideal is alive and real, and its observance by the vast majority of West Point graduates continues until the day they die. I cannot help but think that much of West Point's reputation for producing leaders of unusual quality has to do with this early development of integrity that they unfailingly follow because they would themselves know if they did not.

If you want to build esprit de corps, you must demonstrate integrity like Babe Zaharias as contained in the West Point honor code. If you do, it won't be long before everyone in your organization knows that you can be trusted, that you say what you mean and mean what you say. The members of your organization will demonstrate integrity in dealing with you, and with each other, and the esprit de corps in your organization will soar.

How to Build Mutual Confidence

The *Armed Forces Officer* says that esprit is "the product of a thriving mutual confidence between the leader and the led, founded on the faith that together they possess a superior quality and capability."

If you want to build mutual confidence, I have found that you must demonstrate your real concern for the welfare of those for whom you are responsible.

Demonstrating your real concern gets back to the right priorities that you must have as a leader. First comes your mission or organizational goals. Then comes the welfare of your people. If you are a real leader, your own personal interests come dead last.

Those who follow you will accept hardships, put up with your personal mistakes and idiosyncrasies, and even willingly risk their lives. There are, however, certain conditions. First and foremost, the cause must be worthwhile. Then you must demonstrate the priority of interests that I outlined for you above.

When I first started university teaching, I asked my friend, and then chairman, Dr. Marshall E. Reddick, how he got such high ratings from students on teaching evaluations. "It's easy," he said. "Students will do whatever you ask, even the most difficult assignments, so long as they realize it is to their benefit, and not mine."

Here was a perfect example of applying the priorities of a leader to the classroom. Marshall recognized that a teacher's first responsibility is to impart knowledge and he taught in such a way that it was to the student's benefit. Marshall's own interests came last.

General Patton drove his men unmercifully. As I told you in a previous chapter, to improve discipline he required his men to wear not only helmets, but also ties. And that was in combat! However, Patton also made many mistakes. You probably heard about the incident where Patton slapped and berated a soldier suffering from a combat psychosis. Patton also gave a speech in which he used profanity to a group of mothers whose sons had been killed in the war. In a post-war comment, he seemed to equate Nazis with Republicans and Democrats. These mistakes caused Eisenhower to twice fire this four-star general despite his combat abilities.

You may have heard about these mistakes, or seen them depicted by George C. Scott when he played Patton in the award-winning movie about this famous general. But did you also know that Patton had one of the lowest combat casualty rates of any commander during World War II?

Even as a twenty-nine-year-old colonel during World War I, Patton demonstrated real concern for the lives of his men. On being given command of the first American tank unit by General Pershing he said, "Sir, I accept my new command with particular enthusiasm because with the eight tanks, I believe I can inflict the greatest number of casualties on the enemy with the smallest expenditure of American life."[12]

Patton repeatedly demonstrated a very real concern for his men despite his toughness. Because Patton demonstrated this concern, while he had his priorities right, he developed a very high mutual confidence that led to an unbeatable esprit de corps. As a result, he was victorious and his men loved him despite his foibles.

Get Your Organization to Focus on Contribution

When John F. Kennedy was sworn in as President of the United States he exhorted his countrymen to "Ask not what your country can do for you. Ask instead, what you can do for your country."

John F. Kennedy knew how to get people to focus on the right objective. He pointed out that we could do great things together, if people focused on what they could do rather than what they could get. Unfortunately, President Kennedy was assassinated before most of his goals could be reached. But the esprit de corps which he started continued on long after his death. Through it, we inaugurated civil rights legislation that revolutionized the country, we made the first lunar landing, and we successfully kept Russian missiles out of Cuba.

A switch from gain to contribution is easier than you might think. You see, all of us play one of two games whenever we do anything. One game is "Get All You Can." The other is "Give All You Can." Regardless of which game is played, all players play to win.

You can bet that a group whose members are playing "Get All You Can" has little or no esprit de corps. On the other hand, you can actually feel the positive spirit in a group whose members are playing "Give All You Can."

Which game is your organization playing? If they are playing the game "Get All You Can," you've got to turn them around quickly. If you don't, your organization will have little esprit de corps and perform marginally at best. To get your group to play the game "Give All You Can," you must take positive actions. You must tell them the game, show them the game, and keep score in the game.

To tell them the game is easy: Decide where you want your organization to go. Build a consensus for your goals through discussion and input from your group's members. Decide on a plan of action and make assignments along with milestone dates for accomplishment.

To show them the game is harder: Everything that can go wrong, will go wrong. You will encounter what Clausewitz called "battle friction." There will be setbacks, discouragements, and defeats. You must positively carry on. You must encourage and demand continued contribution and further sacrifice, even in the face of adversity.

Simultaneously, you must keep score in "Give All You Can." That means rewarding the major contributors and sometimes punishing those who are still playing the old game. This is not always easy. Some who contributed something when others contributed nothing during "Get All You Can" continue to play the old game. Frequently they have to be brought to understand the new game.

All the time, you must set the example of being the number one contributor. You need to do without compromise because you won't fool your organization. Not for a minute. The first time that you begin playing "Get All You Can," you can expect your organization to follow your lead the same day.

Once you know that the members of your organization are focused on contributing to its benefit over their own, you won't need to ask if your organization has a high esprit de corps. You will see that esprit de corps with your own eyes, and people will be telling you how happy they are to be in your organization. To build and maintain high morale and esprit de corps, follow these action steps:

1. Let others participate in the ownership of your ideas, goals, and objectives
2. Be cheerful in everything you do
3. Know what's going on and take action to fix or capitalize on it
4. Lead by personal example whenever possible
5. Maintain high personal integrity
6. Build mutual confidence by demonstrating real concern for those you are responsible for
7. Focus on contribution, not personal gain, and encourage everyone in your organization to do the same

In the last two chapters, we've learned how to build a winning organization like a winning football team. You know that to do it requires the construction of four building blocks:

- Cohesion
- Teamwork
- High morale
- Esprit de corps

Construct these four elements, and you'll have an organizational team that can play with the "pros" and win, any day.

Colonel LeRoy P. Hunt, of the United States Marine Corps, had the following message mimeographed and given to his troops just before they landed at Guadalcanal: "We are meeting a tough and

wily opponent but he is not sufficiently tough and wily to overcome us because WE ARE MARINES."[13]

Is there any question about why this team won?

Now turn to the next chapter and see how to coach your
winning team.

ENDNOTES

[1]*The Armed Forces Officer* (Washington, DC: Armed Forces Information
Office, 1975), p. 132.

[2]*Ibid.*, p. 138.

[3]Robert Debs Heinl, Jr., *Dictionary of Military and Naval Quotations*
(Annapolis, MD: United States Naval Institute, 1966), p. 196.

[4]Edgar F. Puryear, *Nineteen Stars* (Presidio, CA: Presidio Press, 1971), p.
19.

[5]*Air Force Leadership* (Washington, DC: Department of the Armed Force,
1948), p. 44.

[6]*Air Force Leadership, op. cit.*, p. 46.

[7]*The Armed Forces Officer, op. cit.*, p. 74.

[8]Edgar F. Puryear, Jr., *op. cit.*, p. 233.

[9]*The Armed Forces Officer* (Washington, DC: Armed Forces Information
Office, 1950), p. 159.

[10]Thomas E. Cronin, "Thinking About Leadership," in Robert L. Taylor
and William E. Rosenbach, eds. *Military Leadership* (Boulder, CO:
Westview Press, 1984), p. 206.

[11]Perry M. Smith, *Taking Charge* (Washington, DC: National Defense
University, 1986), p. 28—29.

[12]Edgar F. Puryear, Jr., op. cit., p. 326.

[13]*The Armed Forces Officer, op. cit.*, p. 160.

Chapter 10

HOW TO COACH YOUR WINNING TEAM

When I was a young lieutenant learning to be a navigator and bombardier in a B-52 aircraft, I had the good fortune to be assigned to a crew on which Lieutenant Colonel John Porter served as the senior navigator.

John Porter had been the "squadron navigator." That is, he was the senior navigator in the squadron. Then the establishment announced a new policy. Staff officers like John were to serve on crews in addition to their staff assignments.

Someone warned me that with Colonel Porter on my crew, I would have to attend the "Porter School of Navigation." This I understood would be neither voluntary nor easy.

Until he was satisfied that you were a straight-shooter, John stood for absolutely no-nonsense. He expected young lieutenant navigators to absolutely know their stuff. Since it was a foregone conclusion that lieutenants did not know everything they should, John was ready, willing, and able to teach.

The next six months of my flying career were far from easy. John demanded and got my full attention both in the air and on the ground. He insisted that I know everything about navigation and B-52s. If I fluffed off, I was instantly corrected. However, when I did my homework, worked hard, but still screwed up, John was patient. He went over things for me and showed me where I had gone wrong. He showed me techniques that increased my ability to operate quickly under the dual demands of time and accuracy.

Ultimately I understood what was meant by the "Porter School of Navigation." It was a term of respect.

Thanks to John's training and coaching, I developed into a passable navigator. His coaching built a team of navigators in the squadron who not only knew their stuff, but were motivated to do their best.

Had we had to go to war during the Cuban missile crisis, much of our ability to carry out our mission successfully would have been because of this one lieutenant colonel.

His example of how to coach led me to become an instructor, and later a combat instructor, and the squadron training officer in attack aircraft in combat in Vietnam.

Some of the teaching techniques I use today, both in the Air Force Reserve and as a professor, came from John Porter.

So thanks, John. I think your coaching in the "Porter School of Navigation" paid off.

A Leader Must Be a Coach and Teacher

There is no question that as a leader you have responsibilities to teach. I mentioned the importance of this concept in earlier chapters. As Major General Perry M. Smith, former Commandant at National War College, says, "Teachership and leadership go hand-in-glove. The leader must be willing to teach skills, to share insights, and experiences, and to work very closely with people to help them mature and be creative. . . . By teaching, leaders can inspire, motivate, and influence subordinates at various levels."[1]

Coaching Must Be a Way of Life

Do you remember the "Kung Fu" television series starring David Carradine? The technical advisor on the series, and also Carradine's double for many of the fight scenes, was a gentleman born in Hong Kong. His name is Kam Yuan. Kam is an engineer as well as a Doctor of Chiropractry. But he is best known for his Kung Fu skills.

Kam and I became friends when I had occasion to do some business consulting for his "Kwoon." A "Kwoon" is a Kung Fu gymnasium. I was most impressed by his sincerity and attitude toward his fellow man. Kam is a person who is always willing to give of himself to help others. He gave of himself even while he ran several businesses, appeared in the Kung Fu television series, made a movie, and instructed in his Kwoon.

At the time, I worked out in another of the martial arts: karate. How, I asked Kam, was he able to maintain his very high standard of Kung Fu, while at the same time having so many other interests?

"Kung Fu," Kam answered, "is not just a martial art, it is a way of life. I practice it continuously."

If you want to coach a winning team, coaching can't be a one-time or even periodic activity. As Professor of Management Burt K. Scanlon says, "Effective coaching is a day-to-day, not a once-a-year activity. The more time that managers spend in a supportive role with subordinates, rather than doing the work or telling them how to do it, the better the results will be."[2]

So if you want to coach a winning team, the first thing you must do is make coaching your way of life. This means that you should look for opportunities to help those who follow you to improve their abilities and skills. The greater the improvement among your group's members, the better they will perform their organizational tasks. The better they perform their tasks, the better the organization you will have.

What to Do to Become a Good Coach

If you want to become a good coach, it's not difficult. There are five things that you must do.

- Be accessible
- Counsel
- Give recognition
- Reprimand
- Discipline

Why You Must Be Accessible

It is a mistake to build a wall between yourself and those you lead. This does not mean that you must become "one of the boys" to the extent that you become overly familiar with them. What it means is that you are completely open with everyone. If there is a problem, or something needs to be said, you want it to get said.

A wall will prevent all but good news from getting through. That can hurt your leadership and your organization quite a bit.

When I was the director of research and development activities for a company, we were trying to develop a set of earcups for flight helmets which would increase the pilot's ear protection. We'd been working for months without success. Finally, we had what appeared to be a breakthrough. The protective results as measured by an acoustical laboratory indicated success. I waited impatiently for my project engineer to approve a general design of the concept. Instead, he looked at the results and said that something didn't look right. He wanted the tests repeated.

I adamantly refused. "After all these months we are finally successful and you want to repeat the tests? No way!"

"Boss, it'll cost very little and will mean only one week's delay."

"We don't need any delay," I countered. "It works now."

"I'm not sure of that," he said.

"Well, I'm sure. Sign the approval."

Fortunately, I had no walls with any of my people. They knew that I expected them to argue their causes as long as they believed in them and until I made a decision. But hadn't I just made my decision?

My engineer looked me in the eye and said, "Boss, if that's the way you want it, I'll sign off. But before I do, I want you to remember that if I'm wrong, the cost is very little. However, if I'm right and these tests are wrong, we'll save a bundle. With that in mind, and before you make your final decision, I want you to know that if we don't repeat these tests I must state emphatically that you're full of bananas." However, he didn't use the word bananas.

His statement caused me to rethink the problem. He was right. I was too eager to press on after so much previous time invested in trying to solve the problem. Since there was doubt, it made sense to take the time to check it out.

We did, and my project engineer was right. The tests were incorrect for several critical frequencies. We had actually solved the overall problem, and this minor problem was easy to correct.

I shudder to think what would have happened had I been the kind of leader who insisted on instant obedience in every situation. We would have wasted $40,000 or more in tooling costs and some time before the error would have been discovered.

Probably more than half of the screw-ups made in any situation that ultimately cause a major problem are actually spotted by someone in the organization. Either this individual was afraid to go to the responsible leader, couldn't get to the responsible leader, or the responsible leader wouldn't listen. The Watergate and Contra affairs as well as the space shuttle *Challenger* disaster all fall into this category.

This doesn't mean that you must always take the advice offered, or that there aren't situations where there is no time for discussion. It means that your subordinates shouldn't be afraid to make their feelings known in the strongest terms possible. It also means that there should be a clear channel to ensure that you receive this message.

Part of this has to do with your manner of dealing with those who report to you. If you accept no difference of opinion, you'll get none.

What do you think will happen if only those who agree with you get promoted? Let me tell you that it won't be long before everyone agrees with you. Some of your best people will have long since left your organization.

You must also frequently check on the procedures in force to allow people to see you. You will find that your staff will tend to protect you from those they consider to be time-wasters or who would upset you. If you make an unthinking comment that you don't want to see any more time-wasters, then you won't. The problem is that it will be your staff's decision as to who is, and who is not, a time-waster.

Counsel Those Who Follow

Counseling means a one-on-one meeting. During this meeting, you can go over what your subordinate has done, good and bad, since the last counseling session. You can also discover what is bothering and what is pleasing the person you are counseling. Sometimes you can find out quite a bit in this way. Along with seeing and being seen, you can keep touch with the health of your organization this way.

There are two important aspects to counseling that you should not ignore. The first is when to do it. The second is what to do in a counseling session.

When Should You Counsel?

Many organizations require that their managers counsel all employees periodically, usually once a year. A periodic counseling is fine. Both you and the individual being counseled knows that it is coming and can prepare for it. For followers or leaders that are reticent about meeting, a periodic counseling insures that a meeting will take place. However, periodic counseling, while good, is insufficient.

In one of my early leadership experiences in industry, I hired an older man who was far more experienced than myself. In many ways, he did a good job. However, one thing that he did drove me up a wall. When I assigned a task, I could not depend on him to complete it on my deadline without several reminders. Of course I reprimanded him. It did no good. He performed well in other ways. He did what I asked. He was not disrespectful. But I had to dun him to get him to complete a project when I wanted it. He could not be depended on to do a job on his own without this nudging. I hadn't the time to let him alone to "learn a lesson" from missing a deadline.

I intended to have a special counseling session with him about this problem, but it seemed that I was always too busy. I knew that after six months his initial salary review with a full counseling session would require me to speak to him in depth. Maybe the fact that he was much older and more experienced than me had something to do with it.

Then the date for his salary review arrived. Now I had a problem. He was doing a good job. But to give him a salary increase when he still wasn't completing projects without reminders meant that I accepted the situation as it existed.

I decided that because of this problem, I could not recommend a raise. However, what I would do was to recommend a supplemental review after an additional ninety days.

At the counseling session, I asked if I had been assigning too much work for him to do. He said that I had not. I explained why he would not be getting a raise and about the supplemental review. I suggested some methods that he might use to insure finishing a project without my reminders. He was surprised. He said that he expected me to remind him continually. According to him, this was the procedure in his former company.

Whether or not his explanation was completely accurate is besides the point. What is relevant is that this employee effortlessly turned the situation around. After our counseling session, I could depend on his getting his work done on time, every time, without me saying anything. He had no difficulty earning a raise at the supplemental review. In fact, I made his raise retroactive to the time of his initial review. I had no difficulties at all with him afterwards.

Here was a case in which I allowed the situation to fester unnecessarily for six months. I vowed that I would never let it happen again, and it never has.

In addition to a special counseling session called for by someone who works for you, you should call for a special counseling session whenever:

- performance is lacking in some way
- you want to get an opinion about something
- you think you can help
- you want to review a past action or project as a learning experience
- you want to offer advise about the future
- there is evidence of a problem of some sort
- any other reason you may have for communicating with someone you work for privately

How Should You Structure a Counseling Session?

Some leaders think that they can easily ad lib a counseling session. This is a mistake. Depending on its purpose, you should clearly lay out what you want to discuss, and what questions you want to ask before the session.

Of course, you should be ready to answer all questions in a straightforward manner. In addition, don't be afraid to ask questions yourself.

Mayor Koch of New York City goes everywhere asking, "How am I doing?" He doesn't always get a positive answer. But every answer provides him with important information about what he and his administration are doing right and wrong in running New York.

Major General Perry recommends that a leader ask these questions during counseling:

- What aspects of this organization do you like the most?
- What areas around here bother you the most?
- What are your ideas for improving this organization?
- What policies, procedures, tactics, subordinate organizations, systems, and so forth should we divest ourselves of and on what kind of a schedule (now, next year, five years from now, etc.)?

- In your judgment, who are the most innovative, helpful, and cooperative people in this organization?
- What are your personal goals while you are in this organization?
- Where and to what job would you like to go next; why and when?
- What do you consider to be your most significant weaknesses?
- What self-improvement programs do you have underway?
- What do you think your chances are for promotion to the next level, and in what time frame?
- What bothers you the most about my decisions and my leadership style?
- What three things cause you to waste your time the most?
- What are the goals that you have established for your organization?
- Please evaluate the performance of the organization, unit, or group that you led over the past six months. Please outline the high and low points of the period.[3]

Note that General Perry's list of questions may or may not be applicable to your organization. So you should not use his list or any list, of questions for counseling without thinking about the peculiarities of your organization.

One successful leader I know follows the same counseling procedure every time he takes over a new organization. He asks each employee, "What is it exactly that you do? What are your problems? How can I help you? What can I do to make your job easier?"

Counseling sessions provide excellent opportunities for subordinates to talk to you off the record, yet in a meaningful way. When you do this correctly, you can find out quite a lot about people that you did not previously know. The biblical quotation, "Ask and you shall receive," is pretty good advice when it comes to counseling.

Your subordinates can talk to you about things that bother them, and you can put rumor and gossip to rest. It is a good opportunity for you and your followers to set goals and work toward performance. Take advantage of this aspect of leadership. Coach your team by good counseling.

Give Recognition

Never fail any opportunity to recognize good performance by someone in your organization. For one thing, it is the right thing to do. When someone does something right, they have earned your praise. Don't you believe that you should be recognized when you do a good job? Don't you feel that you have earned the recognition of others under these circumstances? Let me assure you that everyone else feels the same way. It is a tenant of human nature. In fact, recognition is one of the most powerful of human motivators.

During World War II, an Army Air Force group commander found that he had as many losses because of accidents and poor maintenance as because of the enemy.

When other techniques failed, he established a system of awards for success in maintenance. The awards in themselves were insignificant. They were certificates of merit, scarce items from the post exchange, and forty-eight-hour passes. He gave these awards for the fewest number of aircraft aborting take-off because of maintenance, the fewest mechanical failures of equipment on missions, and the most number of days aircraft were available for combat.

This leader used every technique he could think of to give the widest praise and publicity to winners. He held special award ceremonies. He had pictures taken and sent to hometown newspapers. He wrote special letters of commendation and favorable communication.

The awards may not have been very significant. But the recognition and local fame that accompanied them were considered pretty important. So much so, that you would have thought that each award was worth no less than $1 million.

This group commander soon had an outstanding maintenance record.[4]

As an old Air Force manual on leadership said, "Make allies of human nature's tendencies. Don't 'buck' them as enemies. This desire for success and recognition is one of your most valuable assets in leading."[5]

Major General "Red" Newman, U.S. Army retired, author of two books on leadership and generalship, says, "In command and leadership many qualities, attributes and techniques are required —including drive, force, judgment, perception, and others. But nothing can replace the inspiration and lift that comes from commending a job well done"[6]

Mary Kay Ash, that fabulous woman who built a $300-million-a-year cosmetics company using outstanding leadership techniques, says, "Because we recognize the need for people to be praised, we make a concentrated effort to give as much recognition as possible."[7]

And so she does. Yes, Mary Kay gives away pink cadillacs, expensive fur coats, diamond jewelry, and many, many other tangible awards for top sales. But she does more. Mary Kay gives out ribbons worth pennies, gets people on stage to receive applause, sends out handwritten notes of commendation, publishes three separate magazines (two monthly, one weekly) to recognize superior performers, and personally recognizes and encourages her people whenever and wherever she can.

Mary Kay feels that one of the strongest forms of recognition costs nothing at all. It is simply praise. Mary Kay believes that your praise will help your people achieve success. She calls this principle "praising people to success." Mary Kay knows that people respond to praise and recognition as to nothing else. And so at every sign of success, even a small one, she heaps on the praise.

"I believe that you should praise people whenever you can; it causes them to respond as a thirsty plant responds to water."[8]

You shouldn't be surprised to learn that her concept is psychologically very sound. Famed psychologist B. F. Skinner adds that to get the maximum motivational mileage, you should praise as soon as possible after the praiseworthy behavior occurs.[9]

Yes, recognition can be one of your most important coaching techniques. Even the Emperor Napoleon was shocked at the sheer power of recognition as a motivator. After being told that his soldiers would commit almost any act of bravery for one of the emperor's medals he exclaimed, "It is amazing what men will do for such baubles."

Reprimand When Necessary

A leader cannot always be a "good guy." Sometimes you must reprimand and discipline. If you fail to do so, the offense, whatever it is, will likely be repeated. In addition, you will send a message throughout your entire organization that you do not care, that any performance or conduct is acceptable. Of course, if you do not care, you cannot expect others who would follow you to care.

General Patton advised immediate reprimand for every mistake; when one of his men made a mistake, he let that man know it instantly. Said General Patton, "I cannot kill a man in our combat training, but I can make every man wish to be dead rather than take the wrath of my anger!"[10]

It is interesting to note that Patton's advice is fully in tune with more modern thinking about reprimands. Kenneth Blanchard and Spencer Johnson advise in their best selling book, *The One Minute Manager*: "Reprimand people immediately. Tell people what they did wrong—be specific. Tell people how you feel about what they did wrong—and in no uncertain terms."[11]

When you must reprimand, do so at once. Remember that a reprimand is criticism. So, as pointed out in an earlier chapter, you should reprimand in private. Sometimes your interview with an intent to reprimand brings out causes that justify the actions taken. Then there is no need to reprimand at all, and you will know it immediately. Since you have had the reprimand interview in private, you will embarrass neither yourself nor anyone else.

If you are angry, tell the individual you are reprimanding that you are angry and why. It's okay to be angry. It is not okay to lose your self-control, however. A loss of control means loss of focus on your main objective in performing the reprimand.

When you reprimand, be certain to keep your mind focused on what you are trying to achieve. You do not want to leave him or her hurt, resentful, or frightened. What you do want is for the individual to have the desire to improve on his or her own. Mary Kay's technique of sandwiching the criticism between two compliments as discussed in Chapter 4 is one way to do this. Another way is to follow Blanchard and Johnson's recommendations:

> Shake hands, or touch them in a way that lets them know you are honestly on their side. Remind them how much you value them. Reaffirm that you think well of them but not of their performance in this situation. Realize that when the reprimand is over, it's over.[12]

Administering Discipline

Occasionally, the offense is more serious. You must administer some form of discipline. When you must administer discipline, do it. Don't delay. The longer you delay, the more difficult it will be for you and for the person who must be punished. In addition, a delay can increase the chances of the disciplining action being perceived as unfair.

Always take some form of corrective action when discipline is needed. If you are disciplining partially as a future deterrent, it is the certainty of the punishment that constitutes the main deterrent component, not the severity of it.

In seventeenth-century England, the punishment for highway robbery was death. Today, the punishment for the same crime is several years imprisonment. However, there are proportionately far less robberies. The reason is that the likelihood of being caught and punished is far more certain today.[13]

In the United States, the incidence of robberies is proportionately higher. There may be many reasons for this. However, it is not because the punishment has been reduced. The penalty for robbery was never death in the United States. One reason for the proportionately higher number of robberies in the United States today is because the likelihood of being caught and punished is less likely than it once was.

One very important aspect of discipline is not to administer it, but to achieve and maintain it.

The Latin root of "to discipline" is "to teach." The level of discipline is, as with the level of teaching, what you as a leader make of it. If you want the members of your group to respect their leaders, to respect themselves, and to always seek to perform to the highest standards, they must be taught to do so. This cannot be done instantaneously. You cannot be lax in enforcing performance and then suddenly come on like Attila the Hun.

George Washington said, "To bring men to a proper degree of subordination is not the work of a day, a month, or a year."[14] George Washington knew that the achievement of high standards of discipline is a rough, tough job that takes some time to accomplish.

What he did not say is that once discipline has been allowed to decay, it is ten times as hard for the old leader to rebuild it. This is why leaders that have failed to maintain high standards of discipline are frequently relieved of command in the military, or fired from their civilian positions. It takes a new leader to turn the organization around. A new leader can be a strong disciplinarian and rebuild the organization. The old leader frequently cannot do this.

What Can You Do If Discipline Isn't What It Should Be?

If discipline in your organization has been allowed to wane, what can you do? First, you can set the example for high standards. You can never expect those that follow you to maintain a high standard of discipline if you fail to do this yourself.

Next, pick one area. Focus on that one area alone.

Let's say that your company has a policy that lunch breaks are limited to one hour. Over the years, this policy has become pretty sloppy. Not only are lunch breaks more than one hour, but most are in the neighborhood of two hours.

If you are a new leader, you can make many changes simultaneously. If you are not, you can't. Work on this one problem first.

List all of the reasons why the current action is unacceptable. It's cheating the company. It's unprofessional. Customers who can't get hold of you when they want to aren't serviced properly. It gives the organization a poor image. It sets a poor example for hourly employees or younger managers, and so on.

Decide on the punishment for failing to adhere to the company's rules. This can be docking of pay, working extra hours, and so on, right on up to firing. This is up to you. Just make sure that the punishment is fair and reasonable.

Think through the whole situation. Are there any circumstances that will justify a longer lunch? How will this be handled? Are you being completely reasonable considering everything?

When you're fully prepared, call your group together and tell them the problem and the solution. Be ready to answer any questions. When you know what you are talking about, your group will realize that you are right and be willing to support you. In fact, you'll probably find that those who have stayed within the rules are very happy about your new policy. They may have felt cheated for years because they pulled more than their share of the load because of others taking extended lunches.

Once you have this problem under control, move on to the next one. You'll be walking a fine line. Naturally, you want to turn things around as soon as you can. And you should. On the other hand, if you try to move too quickly after you yourself have been too permissive, you'll cause considerable resentment. This resentment will actually slow your progress and may cause other problems.

But you can do things to start moving things in the right direction no matter what changes must be made. When Thomas H. Wyman took over the Green Giant Company, a company with annual sales of more than $425 million, he found the culture too relaxed. How do you administer discipline to a culture? According to President Wyman, "It's not very complicated. If you call a couple of meetings at 4 o'clock (which will obviously last for an hour or two), that begins to communicate a message. Or you leave a note on someone's desk at 5 o'clock saying you're sorry they couldn't meet with you. You follow up the next day on requests for information. You suggest close-in deadlines. You answer your own mail very promptly."[15]

Six Ways to Coach Your Winning Team

1. Make coaching a way of life. Do it day in and day out.

2. Ensure that you are accessible to those you lead.

3. Counsel those you lead periodically and when they need it.

4. Never let an opportunity to recognize someone for good performance go by without taking it.

5. Reprimand whenever you have to.

6. Maintain high standards of discipline.

Finally, for maximum effectiveness give recognition, reprimand, and discipline as soon as you determine one of these actions should be taken.

ENDNOTES

[1] Perry M. Smith, *Taking Charge* (Washington, DC: National Defense University Press, 1986), p. 4.

[2] Burt K. Scanlon, "Managerial Leadership in Perspective: Getting Back to Basics," in A. Dale Timpe, ed. *Leadership* (New York: Facts on File Publications, 1988), p. 25.

[3] *Ibid.*, pp. 39—43.

[4] *AFM 35—15 Air Force Leadership* (Washington, DC: Department of the Air Force, 1948), p. 23.

[5] *Ibid.*

[6] Aubrey Newman, *Follow Me* (Presidio, CA: Presidio Press, 1981), pp. 176—77.

[7] Mary Kay Ash, *Mary Kay on People Management* (New York: Warner Books, 1984), p. 25.

[8] *Ibid.*, p. 23.

[9] William F. Dowling and Leonard Sayles, *How Managers Motivate*, 2nd Ed. (New York: McGraw-Hill, 1971, 1978), p. 18.

[10]Porter B. Williamson, *Patton's Principles* (New York: Simon & Schuster, 1979), p. 35.

[11]Kenneth Blanchard and Spencer Johnson, *The One Minute Manager* (New York: William Morrow and Company, 1982), p. 59.

[12]Ibid.

[13]*AFM 35-15 Air Force Leadership, op. cit.*, p. 38.

[14]*The Armed Forces Officer* (Washington, DC: Department of Defense, 1975), p. 123.

[15]Chester Burger, *The Chief Executive* (Boston: CBI Publishing Company, 1978), p. 88.

Chapter 11

SECRETS OF MOTIVATION

Why are people motivated to do things for you or for your organization? The truth is there is no one single factor that motivates all of your people all of the time. Also, different people are motivated by different things at any one point in time. But the biggest mistake that leaders make with motivation is not even understanding what motivates most of their followers most of the time. The worst situation is thinking that those who follow you are motivated primarily by one thing, when in fact they are motivated by something entirely different.

Social scientists studied many industries to determine what factors employees consider most important in their jobs. My psychologist wife tells me that over the years, their questionnaires have been given to hundreds of thousands of employees. The results have been known for some time. They are not secret. One recent study was done by the Public Agenda Foundation and noted by John Naisbitt and Patricia Aburdene in their book *Re-inventing the Corporation.*

Before I give you these results, maybe you would like to take the test yourself. I've given it to thousands of leaders in my seminars. All you need to do is to rank the following factors in the order of importance you think your employees would put them. Take a couple of minutes to do this before going on. You can write your ranking order of importance right in the book. Rank each factor in its order of importance to those who work for you, with "1" being most important, "2" being second most important, and so on. Don't look at the answers below until you are certain you have these factors in their order of importance to your employees.

_____ Work with people who treat me with respect

_____ Interesting work

_____ Recognition for good work

_____ Chance to develop skills

_____ Working for people who listen if you have
          ideas about how to do things better

_____ A chance to think for myself rather than just
          carry out instructions

_____ Seeing the end results of my work

_____ Working for efficient managers

_____ A job that is not too easy

_____ Feeling well informed about what is going on

_____ Job security

_____ High pay

_____ Good benefits

Now, go over your answers. Then turn the page.

__1__ Work with people who treat me with respect

__2__ Interesting work

__3__ Recognition for good work

__4__ Chance to develop skills

__5__ Working for people who listen if you have
          ideas about how to do things better

__6__ A chance to think for myself rather than just
          carry out instructions

__7__ Seeing the end results of my work

__8__ Working for efficient managers

__9__ A job that is not too easy

__10__ Feeling well informed about what is going on

___11___ Job security

___12___ High pay

___13___ Good benefits

Why Job Security, High Pay, and Good Benefits May Not Be as Important as You Thought

That's right, the factors are exactly in their order as listed. These are the results after interviewing hundreds of thousands of employees. How many did you get right? Ninety percent of those leaders that I survey put job security, high pay, and good benefits in the top five. That is, they thought that these factors were the most important to their employees. But these three factors are usually far down the list.

Now this doesn't mean that job security, high pay, and good benefits aren't important. They are. But these other factors are more important.

I once worked as an executive recruiter. It was my job to find unique top executives for my client companies according to detailed job specifications that we prepared together. Usually the candidates for these positions were already employed at high positions in other companies. So a good part of the job was convincing these top flying executives that it was worth their time to look at a new opportunity.

Yes, compensation, benefits, and security played a part in their decisions. But even though inducements to move in compensation alone could be 30 percent or more, many executives just weren't interested. For those that were interested, the increased salary and benefits were usually more important as signals that the new job was truly more important and a better opportunity. And yes, some executives left for jobs at lower salaries, fewer benefits, and less job security. This was either because the position presented a greater opportunity to them in other ways, or because they were dissatisfied in their present positions despite the higher pay and benefits.

What Do People Want from Their Jobs?

Go back over the list. Look at items in the upper half of this list. These are:

- Working with people who treat me with respect
- Interesting work
- Recognition for good work
- Chance to develop skills
- Working for people who listen if you have ideas about how to do things better
- A chance to think for myself rather than just carry out instructions

What do these all have in common? Well, for one thing, none of them will cost you very much to implement compared with pay, benefits, or perfect job security. For another, these are factors that you can improve regardless of restrictions or limitations on salary or benefits placed on your organization by your parent organization.

Think about what this means to you as a leader who wants to motivate his people to higher performance. Most of these factors considered important by employees can be improved by you today.

Treating People with Respect Wins Over People and Wins Battles

Isn't it within your power to treat people with respect and insure that others that work for you do the same? Certainly every human being deserves to be treated with respect. Many outstanding leaders maintain you should treat those that work for you with even more than respect. Like Mary Kay Ash, you should imagine everyone you see wearing a large sign saying, "MAKE ME FEEL IMPORTANT."

The night before the Battle of Austerlitz, Napoleon went from campfire to campfire in his army. At every stop, his men gathered around him. Napoleon joked with his men and thanked them for their loyalty. He assured them of victory and explained how he had arranged for medical aid to come to them as swiftly as possible if they were wounded.[1]

Do you think Napoleon treated his men with respect? You bet he did, and you can bet this respect was returned as well.

" 'Promise us,' shouted a veteran grenadier, 'that you will keep yourself out of the fire.'

" 'I will do so,' Napoleon answered; 'I shall be with the reserve until you need me.' "[2]

If You Want People to Go All Out, Make Their Work Interesting

Can you provide interesting work, or can you make the work that your people must do interesting in some way? There are many opportunities to do this if you think about it. This is why making striving a competitive activity can increase the productivity of your organization.

You would think that a battle is just about as interesting an endeavor as you might imagine. How can a battle be made more interesting? Well, English Field Marshall Montgomery found a way. Listen to Montgomery's famous order to his men before the Battle of Al Alamein in World War II:

> The battle which is now about to begin will be one of the decisive battles of history. It will be the turning-point of the war.[3]

Who wouldn't want to do their best in one of the decisive battles of history, in one that would be the turning point of the war? Montgomery motivated his army to top performance and they defeated the Rommel and his "unbeatable" Africa Korps.

The importance of interest in motivation is not a new concept. Almost seventy years ago, Professor Warren Hilton wrote:

> "It is not enough to have a mere general passion for success. Mere indefinite wishing for success will never get you anywhere. Besides this general passion, you must have definite interests continually renewed. You must give the mind something specific and tangible and immediate to work upon. You must incessantly add new details. Otherwise interest, attention, and activity will wane.
>
> Your biggest problem is how to keep your efficient output of mental energy at a high level. The solution lies in maintaining interest. . . . You must continually devise new ways of renewing the interest of your men and inspiring them to concentrate their attention upon . . . the mission. You cannot give a young man . . . monotonous and routine duties to perform and expect him to take the interest that you take in your business. You must make his work interesting for him. . . . Keep his and your interest

alive by trying to discover new things in old surroundings and new aspects to everyday tasks."[4]

Recognition for Good Work Is Only Fair
. . . And It Pays Dividends

How many different ways can you think of right now to recognize good work? How many different awards and rewards can you give to those who work for you? How many different ways can you think of to publicize your followers' success? How many different personal ways can you say "congratulations, we're proud of you?"

Brigadier General Ezer Weizman was commander of the Israeli Air Force in the early 1960s. In those days, the Israeli Air Force was poorly equipped. It was a small Air Force that had not yet gained the reputation for effectiveness which it established only a few years later.

General Weizman knew every pilot in his Air Force by their first name, and that's how he addressed every pilot. He knew every man's personal problems and interests. He sent flowers to every pilot's wife who gave birth. He coined the Air Force's recruiting slogan, "The Best for the Air Force." Whenever he picked up the telephone, his opening sentence was always, "Well, what's news in the best Air Force in the Middle East?" Gradually, his men became convinced that despite their small numbers, they were the best.

War came about a year after General Weizman was promoted to Chief of Operations of the Israeli Defense Forces. His pilots didn't let him down in combat. They destroyed 352 enemy aircraft in the first few hours of the Six Days War.[5]

Make Sure Your People Have the Opportunity to Develop
Their Skills

Do you create the opportunity for those in your organization to develop their skills? Can you provide special courses in-house? How about a few hours off every week to complete a college degree? Maybe you can hire a physical fitness instructor to work with employees during lunch or after work. Sometimes an employee has the ability to do this, or has unique knowledge about something in which he or she is willing to instruct other employees. All you need to do is ask.

Please don't forget the requirement for you and other leaders in your organization to act as teachers.

Of course, by teaching, you also learn. One of the most famous German aces in World War I was a young captain by the name of Oswald Boelcke. Boelcke is especially noteworthy because the tactics he developed more than seventy years ago are still in use by fighter pilots today.

Boelcke went to extraordinary lengths to ensure that new pilots assigned to his squadron were broken in correctly. He would do everything possible to insure a victory for one of his student pilots, and that included giving up an opportunity to run up his own score of airplanes shot down.

It was Boelcke who developed the idea of "Hunting Squadrons." We would call them fighter squadrons today. He was given command of one such squadron himself. Though he spent much of his time teaching, he managed to down forty aircraft. He died fairly early in the war on October 28, 1916, from an aircraft accident. Had he continued to serve, he might have topped the more famous Von Richthofen who lived two more years and died with eighty victories.

Boelcke's teaching probably helped his country's war efforts more than his personal aerial victories. And his teaching might have helped him gain his victories as well, despite lost opportunities. To quote the New Testament: "Thou therefore which teachest another, teachest thou not thyself?" (Romans 2:21).

Listening Motivates

There is little question that listening motivates. It may be far more important in leadership than you ever realized. Recently I had the opportunity to talk about top level military leadership with seven four-star generals and admirals. These were individuals who had reached the very top of their profession before retiring. They had been Chiefs of Staff of their services, Commanders-in-Chief, and one had been Chairman of the Joint Chiefs of Staff.

One of the very few factors that set them off from other highly qualified combat leaders who did not reach the top was their ability to listen. In one way or another, every single one of them mentioned this as an important, if not critical, factor in leadership.

General Bernard P. Randolph is the Commander of Air Force Systems Command. This incredible organization does all of the Air Force's research and development work. This includes all of its advanced airplanes, missiles, satellites, and "Star Wars." In addition to being selected to command an organization that is crucial to the nation's defense, General Randolph is unique in being only the second black Air Force officer to earn four stars. When asked to explain his leadership philosophy in an interview, he answered: "Ask your people what's important to them, and listen. Don't be afraid to make mistakes."[6]

Robert W. Galvin is Chairman of the Board and Chief Executive Officer of Motorola, Inc. His company has $1.5 billion in annual sales and employs 50,000 people around the globe. What does the head of a $1.5 billion company emphasize in his leadership practices? "I emphasize listening," says Chairman Galvin. "We strive to hear what other people want us to hear, even though they don't always come out and say it directly."[7]

Mary Kay Ash maintains that listening is an art. She says: "If I'm talking to someone in a crowded room, I try to make that person feel as though we're the only ones present. I shut out everything else. I look directly at the person. Even if a gorilla were to walk into the room, I probably wouldn't notice it."[8]

Harry K. Wells is Chairman and President of McCormick & Company, Inc., a specialty food company that employs 5,000 people and produces a third of a billion dollars in annual sales. McCormack & Company has earned an international reputation as a company that knows how to listen to its people and integrate even lower level employees into decision making. Says Harry Wells: "Because of an underlying attitude that the company has developed over the years about how people interact, we have an atmosphere that allows anyone here to to sit down and have meaningful dialogues about our policies and our objectives for the future."[9]

Can you create a program to enable you to better listen to new ideas? I'm not talking about the old suggestion box, where a committee that doesn't understand the problem meets periodically and mostly turns down the suggestions made.

Why not go 50-50 on time? Maybe you can donate one hour of company time and your employee can give one hour of time after work to work on his idea using company facilities. Think up some way that the employee will benefit if his or her idea proves useful. That's the way to listen to ideas! I'm sure you can think of additional ways.

Let Your People Think for Themselves

Are you open to letting your people think for themselves? Tell people what to do. Let them decide how to do it for themselves. I don't mean that you shouldn't give help if asked—only that people have their own brains, experiences, and unique backgrounds. That's why they're assigned to the duties that they're assigned to and you are not. That's why they're such valuable commodities.

You can't do all of the thinking for everyone in your organization. Try it and you are sure to fail.

Even if you could do all of the thinking for all of your subordinates, you would be ill-advised to do so. If all of your people thought exactly as you do, your organization would have a rather limited source of ideas.

Perhaps even more importantly, researchers have discovered that the product of many separate brains working together is greater than the sum of each if considered separately. If you try to do all of the thinking in your organization yourself, you will lose this important synergy.

Let those you lead do their own thinking, and you'll be amazed and surprised at what they come up with and how they use their expertise to solve your problems.

Colonel Motta Gur commanded the Israeli paratrooper brigade that captured Eastern Jerusalem during the Six Day War of 1967. There was desperate fighting when Gur, in a vehicle called a half-track, led his paratroopers into the city. His driver was a huge soldier from the Galilee by the name of Ben-Zur.

With Ben-Zur, he passed a column of Israeli tanks and hurried on. At the Lion's Gate to Jerusalem, the entrance was very narrow because of a burning car. Colonel Gur ordered only, "Ben-Zur, drive." His driver continued and without slowing down, managed to avoid the burning vehicle.

As they got closer, they saw that the iron gate had been hit by tank fire and was partially opened. Gur assumed that he would be attacked with grenades as they slowed to open the gate. But he said only, "Ben-Zur, drive."

Ben-Zur stepped on the gas and knocked the door off its hinges. Stones flew in every direction, but the vehicle continued down the Via Dolorosa.

They turned left and found the way blocked by a deserted motorcycle in the middle of the road. The motorcycle could be mined. Gur ordered, "Ben-Zur, drive." Ben-Zur didn't stop and didn't attempt to avoid the motorcycle. Instead, he ran directly over it. If mined, it failed to explode.

Colonel Gur continued in this fashion. At every obstacle, his only order was, "Ben-Zur, drive." The driver made the decision as to how to go over, around, or through the obstacle in order to continue. Eventually Gur, followed by his brigade, arrived at the Temple Mount. For the first time in almost 2,000 years, Jews controlled the Holy Temple.[10]

Colonel Gur eventually became a general and chief of staff of the Israeli Army.

What Does the Military Model Say?

Let's look at our military model again. Why does a private soldier making only several hundred dollars a month make a do-or-die assault on a hill, or drive a vehicle into danger as did Colonel Gur's driver, Ben-Zur?

Colonel Mike Malone should know. He has long been known as the Army's leading expert on leadership. He won the Army's highest peacetime decoration, the Distinguished Service Medal, for his work in this field. According to Colonel Malone, a soldier goes all out in an attack because:

1. his buddies are counting on him
2. he thinks his buddies will call him a coward if he doesn't
3. he has learned that his leader knows the right thing to do
4. he wants to please his leader
5. he believes he will be court-martialed if he doesn't
6. he thinks he will be left alone if he doesn't attack
7. he believes that following orders is the right thing to do
8. he believes that he will be rewarded for attacking
9. he believes that attacking is less dangerous than not attacking
10. he believes that he will feel guilty if he doesn't

11. he wants to prove his manhood, courage, competence, or worth as a soldier

12. he enjoys the excitement and thrill of combat

13. following orders has become automatic [11]

Note that job security, high pay, or good benefits play a very small part here. This is consistent with results that Professors Warren Bennis and Burt Nanus from the University of Southern California found in surveying leaders from all kinds of organizations. You can be a terrific leader in most situations despite poor working conditions, low compensation, and few benefits.

When Are Salary, Job Security, and Benefits Important?

Salary, job security, and good benefits are important. But they are not of primary importance.

You may say, "Listen, in my company people work primarily for the pay and benefits, and that's it." Let's see if that is true.

If you've been in a company for any length of time, you've seen people leave voluntarily. If asked why they are leaving, they will almost invariably respond that they have better offers elsewhere. They may then begin to detail all the advantages of their new positions: higher salaries, bigger jobs, more benefits, bigger offices, and so on.

If you listen carefully, however, you'll hear a message, even if it isn't verbalized. The message is this: "These people who hired me really appreciate what I have to offer. They recognize my real importance to a much greater extent than here. They are giving me all these benefits because I am especially important."

In other words, although the higher salary and additional benefits were inducements to leave an organization, they may only provide the rationale for the real reason.

Recall again that there are many organizations for which pay, benefits, and job security are nonexistent. Yet those that work in these organizations perform to their maximum. Did you forget the football team we talked about in an earlier chapter? There are also voluntary hospital workers, those who work on dangerous archeological digs for low pay, the Peace Corps, the "Big Brother" programs, the Boy Scouts and Girl Scouts, and hundreds of other organizations.

What part then do salary, benefits, and security play in motivation?

What a Scientist Discovered about Motivations
Being Interrelated

Back in the 1950s, a social scientist by the name of Abraham Maslow developed a theory of how all motivations fit together. Maslow called his theory the hierarchy of needs. You may have heard of it before. But let's see how it might affect motivation from a practical viewpoint.

According to Maslow, we are motivated by various human needs. These needs are at different levels. As one level of needs are satisfied, people are no longer motivated by them. People seek to satisfy the next higher level of needs.

Maslow's first level consists of physiological needs like eating or breathing.

Once these basic physiological needs are satisfied, people seek the next highest level. These are security or safety needs. That's where salary, benefits, and job security came in.

On the next level are social or affiliation needs. After this comes the esteem level. Respect and recognition are motivational at this level. Maslow's highest level is self-actualization. That is, to be everything you are capable of being.

Maslow also identified two categories of needs not on his hierarchy. These were the desire to know and understand and aesthetic needs.

Maslow's theory tells us that once people pass a certain level, they are no longer motivated by the levels below. Do you stop and worry about breathing? Not unless you have health problems affecting your ability to breathe. It is the same with salary, benefits, and job security. If an employee has salary, benefits, and job security in amounts he finds acceptable, of itself this may no longer motivate!

Of course, if there is a threat of losing these three factors, they may become motivational once again.

Maslow's hierarchy of needs is important to us because it helps to explain why high salary, good benefits, and job security may not be as important as other motivational factors, except as symbols of these other factors.

Let me show you what I mean. Some years ago, a company I worked with gave a salary review every year. The amount of annual salary raise was keyed to performance. A top performer could get as much as a 10 percent increase plus a cost-of-living adjustment. An average performer received a lower percentage increase for the year. Someone performing below par didn't receive an increase.

One year the company had a very bad year. The company could have frozen all wages. Instead, what it did was to freeze salaries for senior management only. A pot was created and a formula developed for dividing the pot based on the previous year's performance. As a result, a top performer making $20,000 a year received an increase of less than $300 a year!

Still, the increase was a motivator because it was a symbol of high acievement and was not awarded to everyone.

The Man Who Found Two Categories of Motivators that Accomplish Different Things

Another scientist by the name of Frederick Herzberg came along a few years later to build on Maslow's work. Herzberg collected data on job attitude among employees in hundreds of companies. From studying this data, he concluded that people have two categories of needs which affect satisfaction or dissatisfaction with a job.

The first category he called hygiene needs. He gave them this name because these needs serve the function of preventative medicine in the workplace. They prevent job dissatisfaction. They are also distinguished by the fact that these needs are never completely satisfied. You have to keep maintaining them, or you lose performance. You can't increase performance with them. But if your organization is already performing well, you can maintain these high standards with the hygiene factors. Hygiene factors include money, status, treatment, and security.

According to Herzberg, motivators are in the second category that relate to the job itself. These are called satisfying factors. They involve feelings of achievement, recognition for accomplishment, challenging work, increased responsibility, and growth and development. These are the factors that produce job satisfaction; fulfilling the hygiene needs only prevents job dissatisfaction.

How can we use Herzberg theory to help us motivate people to be satisfied with their jobs? We know if we reduce the hygiene factors, we're going to get job dissatisfaction. How would you feel if someone reduced your salary? So to avoid job dissatisfaction, we maintain the hygiene factors at their present levels.

Can we increase job satisfaction by say, increasing salary? No, according to Herzberg. Remember, salary is a hygiene factor. If we want those we lead to be more satisfied with their jobs, we must use the motivators. That is, we must look for ways that we can increase:

- feelings of achievement
- recognition
- challenge in the work
- responsibility
- growth and development

Every successful military leader has done this, and you can do it too. If there is adversity, so much the better.

Have you ever heard of Lewis B. "Chesty" Puller?

Puller is the only Marine in history to win five Navy Crosses. The Navy Cross is second only to the Congressional Medal of Honor. Very few men win one Navy Cross. It is extremely rare for someone to win two. Chesty Puller won five. He quit Virginia Military Institute in 1918 to enlist in the Marine Corps, and fought over a hundred battle in the Banana Wars of the 1920s, in China in the 1930s, and in the Pacific during World War II. He then came out of retirement to fight in the Korean War.

So admired was Puller that marine recruits would sing this little ditty to the tune of "Good Night, Ladies."

> Good night, Chesty! Good night, Chesty!
> Good night, Chesty, wherever you may be!
> After you the Corps will roll, Corps will roll, Corps will roooooll,
> After you the Corps will roll—on to victoree! [12]

In December 1950, Colonel Chesty Puller led a regiment in retreat to the port of Hungnam, Korea. The entire First Marine Division had been cut off by overwhelming numbers of attacking Chinese. The Korean winter was bitter cold and there had been a snowstorm in the morning. There were many wounded. Conditions were grim. Puller stomped up and down the lines. He stopped often to herd men together.

"You're the First Marine Division—and don't you forget it. We're the greatest military outfit that ever walked on this earth. Not all the Communists in hell can stop you. We'll go down to the sea at our own pace and nothing is going to get in our way. If it does, we'll blow the hell out of it."

To others of his own regiment he exhorted, "You're the finest regiment in the finest division in history. We're not retreating! We've about-faced to get at more of those bastards. Be proud your First Marines."[13]

When Chesty Puller finally retired from the Marines permanently, he retired as a lieutenant general.

Action Steps to Motivate Those You Lead

1. Work on the most important factors first. High salary, good benefits, or job security are of lesser importance.

2. Treat those you lead with respect—always.

3. Make the work interesting.

4. Always give recognition for good work.

5. Give those you lead a chance to develop their skills.

ENDNOTES

[1]John Laffin, *Links of Leadership* (New York: Abelard-Schuman, 1970), p. 189.

[2]*Ibid.*

[3]*Ibid.*, p. 265.

[4]Warren Hilton, *Applied Psychology: Processes and Personality* (San Francisco: The Applied Psychology Press, 1920), p. 97.

[5]Eli Landau, "Ezer Weizman," in Moshe Ben Shaul, ed. *Generals of Israel* (Tel Aviv, Israel: Hadar Publishing Co., 1969), p. 72.

[6]"AFSC's New Boss, Gen. Randolph," *Airman* (December 1967), p. 9.

[7]Chester Burger, *The Chief Executive* (Boston: CBI Publishing Company, 1978), p. 48.

[8]Mary Kay Ash, *Mary Kay on People Management* (New York: Warner Books, 1984), pp. 30—31.

[9]Chester Burger, *The Chief Executive* (Boston: CBI Publishing Company, 1978), p. 24.

[10] Arieh Hashavia, *A History of the Six-Day War* (Tel Aviv, Israel: Ledory House, updated), pp. 226—29.

[11] Dandridge M. Malone, *Small Unit Leadership* (Presidio, CA: Presidio Press, 1983), pp. 3—4.

[12] Burke Davis, *Marine!: The Life of Chesty Puller* (New York: Bantam Books, 1964), p. 6.

[13] *Ibid.*, p. 3.

Chapter 12

SEVEN STEPS TO TAKING CHARGE IN CRISIS SITUATIONS

A friend of mine worked as a project manager in his father's $10 million engineering company. He was his father's only son, and had been well educated at one of the country's most prestigious private colleges. However, his father didn't believe in sharing power with a progeny. He felt that there would be plenty of time to train his son to run the company in the future.

Nine years later, when my friend was only thirty years old, his father suddenly died of a heart attack. In one day, he went from middle manager to the top job in the company.

I met this man only five years later. In five years, his company had quadrupled in size. His leadership was heralded by experts, and he and his company were written up in several important business magazines.

How had this unique individual taken charge and asserted his leadership under crisis conditions? How had he managed to do so well?

If you want to know something, there is frequently only one way to find out. That is to ask. So I asked.

"It wasn't easy," my friend said. "First there was the shock over my father's death. Then there was finding out the company's situation. My father hadn't confided in anyone. Everyone had a little piece of the puzzle. No one had the full story.

"The most difficult thing, however, was to assert my leadership. I was now leading people who had been very senior to me in the company. Some had been with the company since before I was born. Not all of them were able to adjust to my style, my goals, or even just me. They refused to accept my leadership.

"I tried to make it as easy as possible for them, and to give them every chance. But when you got right down to it, I was in charge. I had no choice but to fire more than a few.

"Gradually, things got better. People could see that my policies and strategies were working to improve the position of the company. They got behind me completely.

"When I think back to those first few months, I don't know how I did it. It was the toughest thing I had to do in my life. But I had to do it. I had no alternative."

How would you like to take charge of an organization under those circumstances? As a leader, sometimes you don't have any choice.

A Leader Must Take Charge in Crises

When Lieutenant General Bernard L. Montgomery took charge of the British Eighth Army in Africa during World War II, he faced major problems. The Eighth Army had been defeated repeatedly by the German General Rommel and his Afrika Korps. After finally winning a victory, Montgomery's predecessor, General Auchinleck, had been persuaded to attack again prematurely. He had been defeated. There was the possibility of an immediate counterattack by Rommel. The Eighth Army had made withdrawal after withdrawal over the months. Orders were out to prepare for yet another withdrawal. Morale in the Eighth Army was at an all time low. Then Montgomery arrived.

Here's what Montgomery did immediately.

- He cancelled all previous orders about withdrawal.
- He issued orders that in the event of enemy attack, there would be no withdrawal. The Eighth Army would fight on the ground they held. Or in Montgomery's words, "if we couldn't stay there alive, we would stay there dead."
- He appointed a new Chief of Staff.
- He formed a new armored corps from "various bits and pieces."
- He changed the basic fighting units from brigade groups and ad hoc columns to full divisions.

- He initiated plans for an offensive saying, "Our mandate is to destroy Rommel and his Army, and it will be done as soon as we are ready."

Speaking later of the events of his first day in charge, he said, "By the time I went to bed that night, I was tired. But I knew that we were on the way to success."[1]

Only a few months later, Montgomery's Eighth Army attacked at El Alamein and won a major victory. It was the turning point of the war in the North African theater of operations. It helped to eventually gain for Montgomery a promotion to Field Marshal. That's the British equivalent to the rank of full General in the United States. It also won for him the title of Montgomery of Alamein.

What You Need to Do to Take Charge

If you are a leader, there will come a time when you must take charge of a group under difficult circumstances. It may be an old organization that is in trouble. It may be a new organization that you must build from the ground up. It may be an emergency situation. I call these crisis problems, "take-charge" situations. When a take charge situation occurs, will you be prepared to take charge? In a take-charge situation, you must take these steps immediately:

1. Establish your objective.
2. Communicate with those you lead.
3. Act boldly.
4. Be decisive.
5. Dominate the situation.
6. Lead by example.
7. Hire and fire.

Know Where You Are Going—Establish Your Objective

In Chapter 2, we talked about the need for vision. Vision is necessary for leadership under all circumstances. Remember, you can't get where you are going until you know where "there" is. Without vision, you have no "there," no objective.

When Montgomery was given command of the British Eighth Army, he wasn't just told, "Here's your Army, see what you can do with it." He was given a definite objective by his boss, Field Marshal Alexander:

"My orders from Alexander were quite simple; they were to destroy Rommel and his Army."[2] Montgomery believed that having a clear objective was critical.

"I hold the view that the leader must know what he himself wants. He must see his objective clearly and then strive to attain it; he must let everyone else know what he wants and what are the basic fundamentals of his policy. He must, in fact, give firm guidance and a clear lead."[3]

Leaders in Emergency Situations
Must Have Objectives, Too

I recently watched a video tape that was made of my oldest son's plebe class as it went through New Cadet Basic Training at West Point. For probably more than a hundred years, this training has been known as "Beast Barracks." During Beast Barracks, new cadets are taught the basic skills that they must have in order to function as cadets. Among the many skills my son was taught during his field training was pulmonary resuscitation.

One scene on the video tape showed cadets being evaluated in their ability to do this. I was impressed not only in the way they had been taught to perform the resuscitation, but in the positive manner they were taught to give direction in support of the objective of saving life.

As each cadet performed the resuscitation maneuver, he or she would point to an imaginary on-looker and command, "You. Go for an ambulance and return here."

The instructions left no doubt as to which on-looker was being sent and exactly what the on-looker was to do.

What the new cadets were taught is an excellent example of the leader knowing what he himself wants and striving to attain it. West Point is well aware that their cadets may be called upon to lead in circumstances other than on the battlefield.

The first rule for taking charge is to have a clear objective of where you want to go or what you want to do.

Now You Know . . . You Must Communicate
Your Objective to Others

General Patton was a real believer in communicating. So much so, that in training, he kept a microphone constantly nearby. Porter B. Williamson, one his officers during this period, reported:

> Our desert radio broadcasting station had one unusual feature. There was a microphone in General Patton's office and a second microphone was by his bed in his tent. Day and night General Patton could cut off all broadcasting and announce a special message or order from his personal mike. When the music would click off we knew we would hear, "This is General Patton."
>
> Often General Patton would say, "I want every man to be alert tomorrow because we are doing the maneuvers for a lot of brass from Washington who don't know the first thing about tanks or desert warfare. We must show them how wars can be won with speed. I am counting on every man."[4]

General Patton also believed in answering his own phone. In his book, *War As I Knew It*, he says: "In my opinion, generals—or at least the Commanding General—should answer their own telephones in daytime. This is not particularly wearisome because few people call a general, except in emergencies, and then they like to get him at once."[5]

Yes, General Patton knew the importance of communication in taking charge, and he spared nothing to insure that he could communicate with those he led. He wasn't the only one to use this technique.

Admiral Kirk commanded the amphibious landing of the Seventh Army in southern France. He used the ships' public address systems to broadcast the results of each day's operations. Loudspeakers on every ship under his command heard his words. As the landing progressed, he gave his sailors and those soldiers who had not yet disembarked a running commentary of the action. You know that a commander who keeps his men that well informed is in charge.[6]

Norm Lieberman was the project manager working for North American Aviation in charge of the development of the F-100 in the late 1950s. He used the same technique. A public address system was set up in the factory. From his office, he communicated with his engineers and workmen instantly and effectively. I'm told that the F-100 was completed without cost overruns and in minimum time. The Air Force thought quite a bit of the airplane as well. Maybe our aerospace company leaders should use this technique today.

Colonel "Jumping Jim" Gavin, commander of the 505th Parachute Regimental Combat Team, and later a Lieutenant General couldn't communicate with his men so easily. Due to security, he couldn't communicate with his men at all prior to the take-off of his historic combat drop in Sicily during World War II.

How does one communicate with several thousand paratroopers flying in different airplanes without breaking radio silence? Gavin used a different but equally effective technique. After take-off, every man was given a small slip of paper that read:

> Soldiers of the 505th Combat Team:
> Tonight you embark upon a combat mission for which our people and the free people of the world have been waiting for two years.
> You will spearhead the landing of an American Force upon the island of SICILY. Every preparation has been made to eliminate the element of chance. You have been given the means to do the job and you are backed by the largest assemblage of air power in the world's history.
> The eyes of the world are upon you. The hopes and prayers of every American go with you. . . .
>   James M. Gavin[7]

How You Say It Is Important Too

Sometimes how you say something is as important as the message itself. Phrase your remarks in as colorful and interesting a fashion as you can. If you do, your words will spread like wildfire throughout your organizations.

General Patton was certainly an expert at this. If you haven't seen the movie *Patton*, it's worth your time and the price of a ticket just to see George C. Scott faithfully reproducing Patton's dramatic messages.

Few can beat this message to his Third Army on the eve of battle: "Why by God, I actually pity those SOBs we're going up against. By God, I do."[8]

You don't need to be profane to be colorful or dramatic. Some messages are so powerful that they come down to us through the years, long after they were originally uttered. During the Civil War, it was Confederate General Nathan Bedford Forest that said that to win in war you only had to "Git thar fustest with the mostest."

On another day, a subordinate informed General Forest that Federal troops were in his rear. His reply was, "Wall, then we're in their'n."[9]

It was a marine general who commented on his unit's withdrawal from North Korea after his outnumbered division was surrounded and cut-off by Chinese troops in these famous words: "Retreat, hell. We're just attacking in another direction."

You may also be familiar with "I have not yet begun to fight," "Don't fire until you see the whites of their eyes," "Damn the torpedoes, full speed ahead," or "I shall return." All were uttered by leaders in battle in communicating with their men. They had a tremendous impact on the leader's taking charge.

If you want your words to get out fast . . . to be repeated again and again . . . and maybe to go down in history: communicate in a colorful and interesting way.

Be Bold

There is an old saying among pilots. It goes like this: "There are old pilots, and there are bold pilots. However, there are no old, bold pilots."

This adage is intended to discourage younger pilots from foolish, reckless, flying . . . except when necessary. There are most certainly times when bold flying and boldness in general is necessary. If there is an objective you are trying to reach . . . well, then, that's what you are getting paid for as a leader. In some situations, if you fail to be bold, you will not be able to take charge.

Patton was known as "Old Blood and Guts." He was a take-charge, bold, decisive leader. However, he was not reckless. His boldness served a definite purpose. He said: "In planning any operation, it is vital to remember, and constantly repeat to oneself, two things: 'In war nothing is impossible, provided you use audacity.' If these two principles are adhered to, with American troops victory is certain."[10]

Let's look at Patton's two principles again. They form one concept in two parts. Patton refers only to war. But you will find his concept true in all leadership situations. Nothing is impossible if you use audacity. Audacity is no more than a synonym for boldness.

It means that as long as your contemplated actions are not illegal, unethical, or dishonest, you should not be afraid to proceed simply because risk is involved. If you believe you are right, go ahead!

Be a Decisive Leader

People do not like to follow leaders who cannot make up their minds or have trouble coming to a decision. To take charge means coming to a decision and communicating it.

In July 1863, General Meade defeated Robert E. Lee at the Battle of Gettysburg. But because he was indecisive about pursuing Lee, Lee's Army of Virginia was able to retreat across the Potomac River without further harm. If General Meade had pursued Lee immediately, he could have cut the Army of Northern Virginia off before it crossed the Potomac. Lee's Army could have been defeated and the war ended that year. Instead, because Lee was allowed to escape, the Civil War went on for another two years with tens of thousands of casualties.

During World War II, a bomber group suffered excessive losses over several difficult missions. Morale was so bad that higher headquarters actually considered disbanding the unit. If that weren't enough, the group sent eighteen bombers on a mission. They ran into such incredible opposition that only six aircraft returned. Now they were really in trouble.

If you saw the old movie *Twelve O'Clock High*, with Gregory Peck, you saw a fictionalized account which incorporated this true story.

The group commander had to take decisive action, or he knew it was all over. He received permission for a "stand-down" of two days.

The first day he ordered the bar opened and allowed his crews to cope with their depression as best they could. Meanwhile, he and his staff went to work and planned a program of intense activity for the next day. It began at reveille and lasted until evening. There were inspections, drills, target study, and practice missions. Every man worked hard the entire day. By night, they were exhausted and had no difficulty sleeping.

On the following day, more relaxed, they flew a successful combat mission without excessive losses. Over the following weeks, replacements came and were trained, and the group was effective until the end of the war.[11]

Maybe you think that you have trouble coming to a decision because you don't have all the facts. Let me assure you that you will never have all the facts. That's just the nature of leadership. This means that almost all of the time, you must make decisions without knowing everything that would help you to make a decision.

Now it is true that the longer you wait, the more facts you will have. Sometimes it is necessary to wait for important facts before making a decision. But you must weigh the delay against the negative impact. Elements of the situation can change. An opportunity may be lost. Your competition may "Git thar furstest with the mostest." Those who follow you will at best be uncomfortable at not having a decision. If you make indecisiveness a habit, they will not want to follow you.

Some leaders I have seen tell themselves that they are putting off a decision in order to get more facts. But the real reason is that for one reason or another they are afraid to make a decision. Failing to make a decision is also a decision. It is a decision to leave everything to chance or the initiative of others. It is not a sign of a take-charge leader. And it ultimately results in a failure.

To be a take-charge leader, follow the recommendation of W. Clement Stone, the self-made multimillionaire. Stone says that when you feel yourself putting off anything without reason say these three words out loud: "Do it now!"

Dominate the Situation

As a leader in circumstances where you must take charge, you must dominate the situation, or it will dominate you. By this, I mean that you must take positive actions to gain control. You must continue to initiate actions to maintain control.

If you fail to do this, you will spend your time and energy continually responding to the actions of others, or to crises in your environment. In other words, you will spend all of your time firefighting.

There are two reasons for this and they aren't complicated. In any take-charge situation, there is a desperate need for leadership. If you do not take the initiative, someone must fill the leadership vacuum. Someone else will attempt to take-charge. You may be the assigned leader. This other person may not be as experienced, as qualified, or as trained as you. It makes no difference. If you fail to act at once and take the initiative, someone else will attempt to fill the leadership role and you will have to fight to regain it.

The second reason why you must immediately dominate the situation has to do with the environment. If you fail to take the initiative, the environment tends to build up on you. First, you have one problem. Then you have two problems. Now you have yet another. Pretty soon the situation becomes unmanageable.

To Dominate the Situation, Take the Initiative

To dominate any take-charge situation, all that is required is that you take the initiative. In other words, you let others or your environment play catch-up to your actions rather than vice versa.

When Montgomery took charge of the Eighth Army, his predecessor anticipated a further withdrawal in response to Rommel's actions. Montgomery turned the situation around by refusing to withdraw and immediately planning for an attack. Imagine, after one day he went to bed satisfied that he was on the "way to success!"

Other commanders also went to bed happily knowing that they had taken the initiative.

Hannibal, the great Carthagenian general, was attacked by a force more than three times his size in 216 B.C. The Roman general Varro had more than 72,000 men under his command. Hannibal had only 22,000. Hannibal's generals advised an immediate retreat. Instead, Hannibal took the initiative. He designed a plan that encouraged Varro to attack Hannibal's weak center while ignoring his two strong wings.

After Hannibal's center had been pushed back, the Romans were so bunched together because of the strong Carthegenian wings that they could not wield their swords fully. At this moment, Hannibal ordered his two wings to close behind the Romans like gates. His cavalry completed the destruction. It developed into the most decisive battle in the history of warfare. More than 60,000 Romans were left dead on the field of battle.

Note that you can take the initiative and dominate the situation even if you don't initially have it and the odds are against you. Much of taking the initiative has to do with your own perception of the situation.

Winston Churchill reported the following incident about Montgomery in his book *The Hinge of Fate*. Montgomery was on his way to the airport to leave England to take command of the Eighth Army. He was accompanied by General Ismay who was head of the Chiefs-of-Staff Committee. Remember that until Montgomery came, Rommel was considered almost unbeatable.

Montgomery spoke of the trials and hazards of a soldier's career. He gave his whole life to his profession, and lived long years of study and self-restraint. Presently fortune smiled, there came a gleam of success, he gained advancement, opportunity presented itself, he had a great command. He won a victory, he became world-famous, his name was on every lip. Then the luck changed. At one stroke all his life's work flashed away, perhaps through no fault of his own, and he was flung into the endless catalogue of military failures.

"But," expostulated Ismay, "you ought not to take it so badly as all that. A very fine Army is gathering in the Middle East. It may well be that you are not going to disaster."

"What!" cried Montgomery, sitting up in the car. "What do you mean? I was talking about Rommel!"

In his book, Montgomery said, "The good military leader will dominate the events which surround him; once he lets events get the better of him he will lose the confidence of his men, and when that happens he ceases to be of value as a leader."[12]

This is true of any leader in a take-charge situation. You must dominate the situation.

Lead by Example

A very old leadership maxim states that you should be willing to do everything you ask those you lead to do. However, in a take-charge situation, it goes above a willingness. At times, you must actually do everything you ask those who follow you to do.

Colonel Jack Broughton was the chief of operations of an F-105 wing during the Vietnam War. The F-105 had a difficult mission. They attacked North Vietnam and downtown Hanoi. It was the most heavily defended target area in the world. It was protected not only by thousands of ZPU, 23mm, 37mm, 57mm, 85mm, and

100mm anti-aircraft artillery, but also by batteries of surface to air missiles (SAMs). Of course, there were also MIG fighters.

For political reasons, there were more restraints placed on American flyers in the Vietnam conflict than in any other war in which Air Forces were involved. Certain military and political targets were strictly off-limits. In some cases, the enemy was warned prior to an attack. When fired on, there were restrictions on returning the fire if it was coming from civilian structures. If an aircraft was battle damaged and had to jettison its load of bombs in order to get back, the "rules of engagement" limited the sites of those jettisoned to nonpopulated areas. Aircrew had been lost trying to obey these rules and loss rates were high.

A senior air commander is not supposed to fly all the combat missions that his crews flew. But according to Jack Broughton:

> It is important that you know the people you fly with and that you know what they are doing. This does not come from sitting in an air-conditioned office and clucking sternly over unimportant details. It comes from getting hot and sweaty and from getting your fanny shot at. There is no way to shake out people and procedures except by being a part of them. You only learn part of the game when you fly the easy ones; you have to take at least your share of the tough ones. The troops watched that schedule pretty closely. They knew who was leading for effect and who was for real, and they responded accordingly.[13]

Another air commander who led by personal example in a take charge situation was Jimmy Doolittle. As a lieutenant colonel, Doolittle led the first bombing raid of Japan early in World War II. Then he was promoted to general and sent to Europe.

One of the airplanes his airmen were given was the B-26 "Marauder." There had been many problems with the B-26. So many were lost while in training in Florida that the airmen had a saying, "One a day in Tampa Bay." The airplane was known as a "killer" ... of our own men.

In combat, there was a reluctance to use the aircraft to its full potential. General Doolittle was faced with a take-charge situation. He visited one his B-26 groups and listened sympathetically to his pilots' complaints about the airplane. He then asked if he could fly one.

He put it through all the normal maneuvers. Suddenly he "feathered" one of the props. Since the B-26 only had two engines, this means that he was now flying the airplane on only one engine. He landed the airplane on one engine, and then took off again. Still flying with only one engine he repeated all the maneuvers he had done previously. Finally he landed.

"Well," he told his pilots, "it isn't the best airplane that America can build, but I think it can do the job."

The B-26 went on to rack up a tremendous operational record in combat during World War II.[14] General Doolittle went on to become the first reserve officer promoted to four-star general.

Parachute General James Gavin jumped with his division on the "D-Day" invasion of Normandy. Young Colonel George S. Patton led his tanks on foot against the enemy during World War I. As a brigadier general in the same war, MacArthur went forward with the first line of his men in the attack. Major General Moshe Dayan of the Israeli Army came under direct fire while up front in an attack during the Sinai Campaign of 1956. His jeep driver was killed. Dayan was Chief of Staff at the time.

All of these men were in take-charge situations. It was time to lead by personal example, and they did.

Hire and Fire

In a take-charge situation, you don't have time to fool around. You must get rid of those individuals that are performing poorly, and you have to replace them with people who can do the job.

For most people, firing is not an easy thing to do. Those you must discharge may have worked at a job for some time. They may or may not have done their best. Either way, firing can mean a loss of money, prestige, security, and sense of self-worth. Still, if you are going to be true to yourself and to your organization as a leader, you have no choice.

Remember, we're not talking about ordinary day-to-day management. We're speaking about take-charge situations. If your organization has a worthwhile purpose and mission, it must come first under these circumstances.

This is easier to see in warfare, where the acts of people spell the difference between life and death, victory and defeat. It is more difficult to understand in peacetime situations.

What harm is it if you keep people on board who are not performing up to standard? First, these individuals are probably incapable of doing any better than they already have. Otherwise, the take-charge situation wouldn't exist. Also, it is essential to get people in important positions who can do the job as you want it done. You can't do this with incumbents occupying the key positions. Finally, you can't motivate others to go all out in a crisis when you demonstrate that you are willing to accept less than the very best from others.

Now I want to make certain that you understand fully what I am saying. Just because you are a leader doesn't mean that you fire everyone in sight that you think you can replace with someone better. That's not ethical. It demonstrates poor leadership. There may well be situations that are not crises when, for various reasons, you should tolerate people in your organization who are not performing up to your standards. One example is an individual who is no longer capable of turning in top performance, but who has done a good job in the past. If possible, you should first attempt to save the person from being fired. You do this through counseling and the coaching techniques that we've discussed earlier.

But in a take-charge situation, don't waste time.

Guidelines for Firing

If firing needs to be done, do it at once. Here are some guidelines:

- Don't mess around with half-way measures or second chances. Make the decision to fire, and do so at once.
- Don't delegate a firing. Do it yourself.
- Don't fire in public. Call the person into your office and do it privately.
- Be forthright and tell the person why he or she is being fired.
- Let the person know that you're not saying he or she is incompetent at *any* job, only that your standards for *this* job have not been met.
- Depending on who is being fired, and at what level, get additional help before you act, if required. That is, you may want to talk to your legal people, public relations, the human resources department, an outplacement firm, a psychologist. Or no one. Only you can decide if you need additional help.

Hiring Is Just as Important in a Take-Charge Situation

When Lee Iacocca turned the Chrysler Corporation around, it was the biggest most amazing turn-around situation in this century. Everyone said it couldn't be done. But Iacocca went ahead anyway. If you think it was just the famous government guarantee on a loan that made things come out, you would be dead wrong. Iacocca did it primarily with people. Like General George C. Marshall, he tracked the careers of several hundred executives in his organization. These were kept in a special notebook. So important was this notebook, that he obtained special permission from William Ford, president of the Ford Motor Company, to take the notebook with him.

Many of the new executives he brought to Chrysler came from this notebook. According to Iacocca, "In the end, all business operations can be reduced to three words: people, product, and profits. People come first. Unless you've got a good team, you can't do much with the other two."[15]

This should tell you clearly that you should be directly involved with hiring executives that will work with you. If you have a notebook of executives yourself, congratulations. Most leaders aren't so well prepared. But don't worry if you do not. You can learn a lot through the interview process if you do it right.

The problem most leaders have in putting their team together in a take-charge situation is that they are not prepared for the interview. They ask one or two questions, and if everything seems okay they offer the job. After all, this is a take-charge situation, right?

It may be a take-charge situation, but this is the wrong approach to take. You see, in a take-charge situation you want to get rid of the deadwood instantly. But it is possible to replace poor performers with worse performers, or individuals just not suited to the job you want them to do.

General Perry M. Smith put together a wonderful checklist to help you to hire the right person for the right job . . . to get a feel for the individual and for the chemistry between you and your prospective subordinate. Here are the questions that he recommend that you ask:

- Do you want the job? Why?
- What talents, qualities, and strengths would you bring to this job?
- What are your weaknesses?

- How long would you like to hold this job?
- What is your leadership/management style?
- If I asked a subordinate of yours to describe you and your leadership style, what would be the response?
- If you are not selected, whom would you recommend for this job?
- What are your long-term personal goals?
- Do you expect to be promoted soon?
- Are there any "skeletons in your closet"?
- Whom in your present organization do you admire the most, and why?
- What is the standard of integrity in your present organization?
- Are you considering any other positions?
- If I select you for this job, would you take it as your first choice over other positions you are considering?
- Are you approaching a retirement decision soon?
- How many people have you led or supervised in your career?
- Have you ever fired anyone? Have you ever been fired?
- What experience do you have with
  —operations?
  —planning?
  —finance?
  —marketing?
  —engineering?
  —research and development?
  —manpower and personnel?
  —computer systems?
- Have you had any setbacks in your career?
  —If so, what were the most significant lessons learned from the setbacks?
  —What organizational setbacks have you observed firsthand?
- What is the toughest problem you have ever faced in your professional career? How have you handled it?[16]

I'm not saying that you must ask all of these questions during the hiring interview. You should ask only those that you consider relevant to the situation, and of course, you should feel free to add some of your own questions that you consider appropriate.

The point is, take the time when hiring in a take-charge situation to put together the best possible team that you can.

Seven Steps to Taking Charge in a Crisis Situation

1. Establish your objective at once. You can't lead anyone anywhere until you know where you want to go.

2. Communicate what you want done in a way likely to get the attention of those you lead.

3. Act boldly. This is no time to be cautious. This is the time to take risks.

4. Be decisive. Don't put off making decisions.

5. Dominate the situation by taking the initiative. If you don't, the situation will dominate you.

6. Lead by example. Make your motto "follow me," and live by it.

7. Get rid of people that can't do the job and hire people that can. Do a thorough job of interviewing to minimize the risk of a bad choice.

ENDNOTES

[1] Montgomery of Alamein, *The Memoirs of Field Marshall Montgomery* (New York: World Publishing, 1958), p. 94.

[2] *Ibid.*, p. 93.

[3] *Ibid.*, p. 75.

[4] Porter B. Williamson, *Patton's Principles* (New York: Simon & Schuster, 1979), p. 31.

[5] George S. Patton, *War As I Knew It* (New York: Pyramid Books, 1966), p. 309.

[6] *AFM 35-15, Air Force Leadership* (Washington, DC: Department of the Air Force, 1948), p. 23.

[7] James M. Gavin, *On To Berlin* (New York: The Viking Press, 1978), p. 18.

[8] *Ibid.*, p. 32

[9]*Ibid.*

[10]George S. Patton, *op. cit.*, p. 308.

[11]*AFM 35-15 Air Force Leadership, op. cit.*, p. 30.

[12]Bernard L. Montgomery, *op. cit.*, p. 75.

[13]Jack Broughton, *Thud Ridge* (New York: J. B. Lippincott Company, 1969), p. 30.

Chapter 13

SEVEN ACTIONS TO DEVELOP YOUR CHARISMA

Charisma comes from a Greek word meaning a beautiful gift. This implies that it is something that you are given. The further implication is that this is done at birth.

Napoleon Bonaparte didn't see it that way. He said: "My power is dependent upon my glory, and my glory on my victories. My power would fall if I did not base it on still more glory and still more victories. Conquest made me what I am; conquest alone can keep me there."[1]

What Napoleon was saying was that his being perceived as a charismatic leader was based on his success. To maintain his charisma, he had to continue to be successful. There is some truth in this. Warren Bennis and Burt Nanus, the two researchers from the University of Southern California we spoke about in earlier chapters, found that successful leaders tend to be viewed as charismatic.

Again, this says that if you want to be a charismatic leader, you must first become a successful one. I don't know about you, but I have a problem with this, even if it does contain an element of truth. What if you don't want to wait until after you are successful to be a charismatic leader? Won't being charismatic help you to become a successful leader? Are there any actions you can take to become charismatic before you become successful? Happily, there are.

The Charismatic Leader

Not too long ago, I was fortunate in being selected to attend the Industrial College of the Armed Forces at the National Defense University in Washington, D.C. The Industrial College of the Armed Forces trains selected senior military and civilian officials destined for positions of high trust and leadership in the federal government.

Prior to a student beginning his or her studies at the National Defense University, detailed leadership evaluation surveys are sent to a number of the student's subordinates, superiors, and colleagues. The subordinates complete these surveys anonymously. Each survey contains 125 questions in twenty-one major areas having to do with the student's leadership abilities, attributes, and characteristics.

Those selected as students for National Defense University are already proven leaders. As you might expect, these leadership evaluations are generally pretty favorable.

In the year I was at National Defense University, the scores for 995 questionnaires for 115 students at the university averaged above 4.00 out of 5.00 for all characteristics measured.

The expected average for a population of leaders is 3.0. Thus above 4.00 means that those surveyed thought that these leaders demonstrated every single one of twenty-one major areas of leadership fairly often. This is much better than the average leader.

The average in the "charisma" area for the 115 students was 4.32. That's an amazingly high score. But one individual's score was off the chart. Every single one of his subordinates had scored him in this leadership area as a perfect 5.00! Translated, it said that every single subordinate felt that this leader demonstrated charisma frequently, if not always.

Eagerly, I sought this individual out to discover the secrets of his unusual evaluation in this mysterious quality. I found an average looking man of average height. If you had met him and did not know of his charisma score, you would not have suspected him of anything special.

What was his secret? He maintained that a great deal of his success as a leader was his being perceived as charismatic. In other words, it wasn't that he was successful as a leader first. He did agree that once he was successful, being perceived as charismatic was a lot easier. However, according to this man, he became successful as a leader partially because he *was* charismatic. More importantly, his charisma was not accidental. He intentionally set out to develop it. Further, he took definite actions to develop his charisma again in every new group which he led.

To develop his charisma, he took several different actions. Over the years, I observed that other leaders who are perceived to be charismatic act in a similar fashion. Here are the actions that they took and that you can take to develop your charisma too:

1. Show your commitment

2. Look the part

3. Dream big

4. Keep moving toward your goals

5. Do your homework

6. Build a mystique

7. Use the indirect approach

Let's see what each action entails.

Show Your Commitment

If you want to be perceived as charismatic, it's not enough to be committed to whatever it is you are trying to accomplish. You must show your commitment to those you lead.

Several historical military leaders have burned their boats after landing for an assault from the sea. Usually their biographers indicate this is done to give their followers "no alternative." The apparent message is that they must win, since they can no longer return to the sea.

I do not think this is the main reason for this action. The attacking troops could still surrender if they wished. I think the real reason that these leaders burned their boats is that it was an extremely effective method of demonstrating the leader's own commitment to the goal or objective.

There are many ways to demonstrate commitment. These include being persistent in the pursuit of a goal, going to extraordinary lengths, self-sacrifice, risk taking, and the expenditure of personal resources.

Do you perceive the founding fathers of our country to be charismatic? They demonstrated commitment in all of these areas. They committed their "lives, fortunes, and sacred honor" to the goals of the group.

How a Man Demonstrated Commitment that Helped
Make Him a Millionaire

Joe Cossman is a multimillionaire. Today, he lives in Palm Springs, California, and by his own choice travels around the world helping people start their own businesses. But he was born poor.

After service during World War II, Joe got a job in Pittsburgh, Pennsylvania, working for an export company. Not being a college graduate or having any special skills, he earned the princely sum of $35 a week. After supper every night, he wrote letters from his kitchen table to contacts he had made around the world. He wanted desperately to export products on his own.

He spent more than a year writing hundreds of letters, following false leads that went nowhere, and giving up all his free time to this activity. Remember, this kind of persistence demonstrates commitment.

One day he saw a small ad in *The New York Times* advertising cases of laundry soap, which at that time was scarce. He confirmed the availability of the soap by telephone, and sent letters to his contacts abroad.

Several weeks later, he was notified that his bank had received a letter of credit for $180,000. This meant that he would receive the $180,000 when he produced bills of lading that the soap had been loaded on board a ship. The letter of credit gave him thirty days to do this. If he failed to supply bills of lading within thirty days, the letter of credit would be worthless.

Joe's soap wholesaler informed him that he had the soap in New York City. All Joe had to do was to get to New York to make the financial and shipping arrangements. Joe approached his boss and asked for several weeks of leave of absence from his job. His boss refused. Joe then went around Pittsburgh and offered friends 50 percent of the deal to anyone who would go to New York City to put the deal together. No one was willing to accept Joe's offer.

In desperation, Joe approached his boss again. If he couldn't get the time off, he would quit. His boss saw Joe's commitment and gave in. Joe and his wife had a total of $300 savings in the bank, but Joe's wife knew his commitment also. She had faith in him. They took the $300 out of the bank and Joe headed for New York City.

After checking into his hotel, Joe again called his soap wholesaler. The number had been disconnected, and the wholesaler was nowhere to be found. But Joe was still fully committed.

He went to the library and found lists of soap companies in the *Thomas Register of Manufacturers*. Returning to his hotel room, he began calling soap companies all over the United States. After running up a phone bill of more than $800, he located a company in Alabama that had the soap. But he would have to come to Alabama to pick it up.

Joe searched all over New York for a trucking company that would go with him to get 3,000 cases of soap, and do so on credit. At this point, he began to have another problem. Much of the thirty days had gone by. Could Joe bring the soap to New York in time?

Joe continued to demonstrate strong commitment to his goals. Those who lent him money would have said that there was just something about him that led them to believe that he was going to succeed.

He got the soap to New York City with less than a day to load the soap on the ship. The unions weren't as strict in those days, and Joe himself helped load the soap. They worked all night. By noon the following day, it was clear that they weren't going to make it by the time the bank closed. With less than an hour before closing time, Joe abandoned the loading dock to look for the office of the president of the steamship line.

As Joe told me, "I hadn't bathed in more than a week. I hadn't slept all night because of helping to load the soap. I was unshaven and had been borrowing small change from the truck drivers for lunch. The soap company was after me for the money for the soap, the trucking company for the money I owed them. The hotel didn't know where I was, and they wanted their money too. Even my wife didn't know my whereabouts. I looked and felt like I could use a case of that soap, myself."

In this condition, he barged into the office of the president of the steamship line and told him the whole story. The president looked Joe straight in the eye. Joe's commitment must have come through. "Cossman," he said, "if you've gone this far, you're not going to lose the deal now."

So saying, he gave Joe bills of lading, even though the soap was not fully loaded. This meant that his company assumed the risk of loss for the soap until the loading was complete. He also had his personal limousine take Joe to the bank.

On this first successful business deal, Joe made a profit of $30,000. That's not bad for a man who had been making $35 a week

How was Joe able to lead and successfully influence everyone that he came in contact with on this business deal? Joe was committed. His commitment was compelling. It was read by others who followed his leadership as charisma.

Roger Ailes, a top media consultant who has consulted for a number of CEOs and political campaigns, says: "The essence of charisma is showing your commitment to an idea or goal."[2] If you want to be perceived as charismatic, think of ways to show your commitment.

Look the Part

A few years ago, a man did serious research on the effect of what you wear has on your success on the job. The results were so astounding, that his book, *Dress for Success*,[3] became a nationwide best seller. John T. Molloy's research demonstrated conclusively that what you wear is important in becoming successful in what you do. If you are in business, you might want to pick up a copy of this book. For most jobs in the United States, Molloy's advice can be extremely valuable.

However, you should know that what kind of leader you are and who you are leading can call for different types of dress for maximum effectiveness. You wouldn't be perceived as much of a charismatic leader if you tried to lead ranch hands in a business suit. In some countries businesspeople do not dress in the way businesspeople dress in the United States.

Also, the way you dress should be carefully built around the particular image of the kind of leader you represent.

The military has recognized this for a long time. Generals frequently design their own uniforms for the image of themselves they wish to portray.

Field Marshal Montgomery was known for his special beret on which he had fixed the emblems of the major units which he commanded. He also made a pullover sweater a part of his uniform. He effected a casual image, even in the heat of battle. When soldiers saw someone wearing a multi-emblemed beret and casual sweater, they instantly knew it was their commander.

Patton also strongly believed in "looking the part." His special uniform consisted of a shiny helmet, pistols on both hips, and a knotted tie, even in combat! Few of his soldiers could mistake him either.

Eisenhower invented the special short military jacket that he wore. Eventually the entire U.S. Army adopted it. They called it the "Ike Jacket."

MacArthur affected a different image. He started wearing a special uniform even as a young colonel in combat during World War I. He refused to wear a helmet or carry a sidearm. He stated his reasoning as: "A helmet hurts my head, and decreases my effectiveness as a leader. I don't carry a sidearm because it is not my business to fight, but to direct others in fighting."

During World War II, his tieless khaki uniform, gold braided hat, corn cob pipe, and sun glasses became famous as a symbol of the MacArthur mystique.

Many other military leaders have looked the part by their dress. Some have worn standard uniforms, but had them tailored and made of better material than the standard. Some commanders carry a "swagger stick." This is a short cane-like affair that could be described as the American version of a marshal's baton. General Matthew Ridgway, commander in Korea after MacArthur's relief, always wore grenades over his winter greatcoat. Brigadier General Robin Olds, F-4 commander and ace in Vietnam, wore a nonregulation oversized mustache. His pilots loved him for it.

My classmate, Colonel "Tex" Turner, Director of Military Instruction at West Point, wears camouflaged battle dress even in the classroom environment. Tex, who formerly commanded the U.S. Army's Ranger School, is a tiger leader, and he makes sure that he looks the part. The cadets feel that Tex can walk on water.

The Commandant of the Marine Corps, four-star General Alfred M. Gray, also wears camouflaged battle dress . . . even in the Pentagon. To my knowledge, he is the only one of the Chief of Staff ever to do so. You can't miss him when you see that uniform. It says, "I am a warrior, and Service is a fighting outfit."

You don't need to wear battle dress, but if you want to appear charismatic, you must take the time to define the image of your type of leader and then dress that way.

Two hundred years ago, Joseph Joubert said: "A well-dressed soldier has more respect for himself. He also appears more redoubtable to the enemy and dominates him; for a good appearance is itself a force."

Dream Big

In an earlier chapter, I showed you why you must have high expectations. I hope I demonstrated to you that you can achieve no higher than you expect to achieve. It is the same in setting goals for others or for a group. There is one additional important thing you should know. No one wants to work hard or make sacrifices for small goals. And why should they? They can reach small goals any day by themselves. They don't need you. Accomplishing such goals means nothing. They aren't exciting. They give no great feeling of accomplishment when achieved. However, if you show those you lead difficult goals, big tasks, and truly worthwhile missions, they will sacrifice everything in order to help you achieve them.

Dr. Charles Garfield observed an extraordinary leap in performance among engineers, workers, and production people in a major aerospace corporation that was building the Lunar Excursion Module for Apollo 11. "Every week, I heard stories about people who were lifting their performance to levels that none of them would have predicted a few months before,"[4] he said. This continued during the entire period of preparation for the moon mission. Then on July 20, 1969, Neil Armstrong and Buzz Aldrin walked on the moon. It was over. People's performance returned to their normal average level. "They had risen to a peak; then they had fallen back to earth," said Garfield.[5]

To maintain performance, the leaders of this company should have immediately gone on to the next big dream. For as long as you ask for really big things, nothing is impossible.

Have you heard of Dr. Robert H. Schuller? Dr. Schuller is a minister, who is also the author of more than twenty books and many cassette tapes, and who has his own television show. He came to California with no congregation and only $500. Twenty-five years later, he built the $20 million Crystal Cathedral, which seats 4,000. Millions listen to his sermons every week.

Dr. Schuller preaches what he calls "possibility thinking." He says emphatically that you can accomplish the impossible. According to Dr. Schuller, it's only a matter of finding the right person to help you.

People will help you to reach goals that are impossible. In fact, they will give you their blood, sweat, and tears, as Winston Churchill demanded, if your goal is big enough.

What kind of goal should you have? It can be anything, as long as it is big and worthwhile.

In his book *Battle Cry*, Leon Uris wrote a fictionalized account of his own experiences in the marines during World War II. His hero, Lt. Colonel "High Pockets" Huxley, marches his battalion on a grueling twelve-hour march to set a divisional training record. With difficulty, bruises, and bleeding feet, they make it and set the record. Then instead of taking trucks back to camp, Huxley orders a few hours rest and then a return march back. His men come near to collapse, but as they rest at the side of the road, they see the other marine units returning to camp by truck after their treks. That they are being made to do something big and difficult inspires Huxley's battalion for one final effort. They make it back to camp and beat their own record at the same time.

At the Battle of the Bulge, the 101st Airborne Division was cut off and surrounded by superior numbers of attacking German units. Who would come to the rescue? Patton announced that he would disengage from the enemy on one front, march a hundred miles, and be in action with three divisions within forty-eight hours. Patton knew that if he demanded the just barely possible, that if it was a really important, tough job, his men would come through.

If you want to develop charisma, remember the words from the song "High Hopes" sung by Frank Sinatra. You may not think that an ant can do much with a rubber tree plant, but if he has high hopes, then: "Whoops! There goes another rubber tree plant!" Have big dreams and foster high hopes among those you lead, and your charisma will never be in doubt.

Keep Moving Toward Your Goals

Having big dreams and goals is important, but you can't let it rest at that. You must actually keep moving toward the tough goals that you have set. Remember, you're the leader. People don't move until you move first. When you do move toward a big dream, it will have a marvelous effect on those you lead. Your backers will be pleased. "What did we tell you," they'll say to others. Then there will be those who were on the fence. They supported you, but they could have gone either way. "We knew he could do it all the time," they'll say. Then there are those who were against your big dream. They said that it couldn't be done. They won't say much. They'll only mutter, "Well I'll be damned." And your charisma will increase among all concerned.

Moving toward your goals is tougher than just setting the goal, but it isn't all that difficult. First, it means that you have to have a plan. We'll see how to do that in the next chapter. Then you set a number of intermediate goals. Dr. Schuller didn't start out right away building the Crystal Cathedral. He set his overall goal and then accomplished a number of intermediate objectives. Every big goal has a number of smaller, intermediate objectives that are accomplished first. Every objective has a number of tasks.

To show movement toward the big goal, know what the intermediate objectives and the tasks are and make certain those you lead know as well. Assign these tasks to a specific individual, and supply a time schedule for when you expect a particular task to be accomplished. Then, check periodically to see what's happening. Publicize every success, every movement toward your big goal. When those you lead run into problems, give them the help they need in order to proceed. Never stop progressing toward your goal. Whatever your goal is, maintain progress toward it. Then, like Joe Cossman, few can resist your charm, and those you lead will comment on your charisma.

Do Your Homework

Did you watch the gymnasts on television during the Olympics? Incredible, wasn't it? Many of the performances seemed flawless. What was even more amazing in many cases was that it appeared to take no effort at all to do something you or I couldn't have done in "a million years." The fact is, however, that those we watched turn in such marvelous performances are made up of the same stuff as you and me. When they first started out, they couldn't do any of those things either. It would have been beyond their wildest dreams. Yet, there they were doing incredible things and winning well-earned medals for their accomplishments.

How do I know this? Because it happened to me, and I know the secret first-hand.

When I was a boy, I had recurrent rheumatic fever. As a result, as I grew up I couldn't participate in sports. I was generally weak. At age fifteen, I knew that I had to get strong if I was ever to get to West Point. West Point required a minimum of six pull-ups—I couldn't do one. Over the next two years, I worked hard to prepare myself, and the result was that I overcompensated. When I took the test at age seventeen, I did fifteen pull-ups.

When I got to West Point, all new cadets who had demonstrated more than average upper-body strength were screened for the gymnastics team. The reason was that very few Army gymnasts had previous experience with the sport before coming to West Point. The gym team needed whatever it could get.

I managed to make the team as a rope climber. Rope was a very simplistic event. You sat on the floor with your arms stretched above your head and your hands clenching the rope. When you felt ready, you exploded off the floor and climbed hand over hand, without the use of your legs. At the top of the rope, twenty feet off the ground, was a circular pan coated with charcoal. You reached out with one hand and made a swoop at the pan. You were timed by three timers from the moment you left the ground until you touched the pan.

An acceptable time for completing the climb was something under four seconds. The best time I could manage my first year was about six seconds. That was not very good, but it was the best I could do. But every day I did my homework. This consisted of climbing the ropes again and again while wearing weight belts weighing about twenty pounds. I have never seen such a direct relationship between work and progress. So week by week, I could see my time getting just a little bit better.

At the end of my first year, someone jokingly asked me if I was going to set a record. By then, I knew that the secret of improvement was practice. I answered that I would, but not until my last year.

Three years later, I climbed the rope in 3.4 seconds. Further, climbing had become so much easier. I could repeatedly climb twenty feet on a rope in less than four seconds and not even get winded. It felt like no muscular effort at all. The feeling was that of a balloon carrying me upward. People who watched me said I climbed "effortlessly." What made the difference between a record-setting climb and just a good climb was only how fast I could move my arms without a hand missing its grasp for the rope. It was always exactly eight strides and a lunge with my free hand for the charcoal-coated pan. The secret for the difference between my early poor performance and my later outstanding performance was simply one thing: homework.

It is the same thing with charismatic leadership. Those who see you perform see only the effort you make on the spot. They don't see the hours and hours of homework that you have put in. Yet, if you do something difficult apparently without effort, you will be perceived as charismatic.

Doing your homework can make your reputation for a lifetime as a charismatic leader. At the Battle of Chippewa during the War of 1812, British General Phineas Riall attacked with 1,700 regulars and about 700 Indians and Canadian militia. He headed for Winfield Scott's brigade. Riall identified them as militia by their gray uniforms. He had beaten this militia, and saw them break and run in previous engagements.

Winfield Scott commanded this militia. He was still a young man in his twenties. What Riall didn't know was that Scott had done his homework the previous winter. He had drilled his militia until they were ready to drop, but now they knew their stuff.

Under fire from Riall, they formed their line effortlessly. With parade-ground precision, they moved to meet Riall with bayonets.

Riall stared at the advancing Americans in amazement, and uttered a tribute to Scott's abilities which has come down through the years: "Those are regulars, By God!" Scott drove Riall back with heavy losses. He became a general before the age of thirty, and eventually General-in-Chief of the U.S. Army. But the homework Scott did prior to the Battle of Chippewa was the original source of his charisma.

Build a Mystique

Have you ever seen a magic show? The magician's tricks may be grand and involve the disappearance of elephants or the freeing of the magician after being chained in a locked trunk and lowered under tons of water. Or the tricks could involve simple cards or coins. The size of the trick doesn't matter. What does matter is that we are fooled. Most magicians seem to have charisma because we don't understand how he or she is able to do the tricks. This gives the magician a certain undefinable mystique. Magicians never tell you how they do their tricks, because they know that to do so would mean a loss of some of their mystique.

Sure, we know we are being fooled. It doesn't matter. The magician knows how to do something that we don't, and he or she does it with an aura of mystery and charisma.

When someone seems to know how to do something that we cannot comprehend, we follow them eagerly. Somehow they seem to possess a special quality that arouses both loyalty and enthusiasm.

If we think a person has a secret of how to do something, that person can attain a certain measure of charisma even after he or she is long dead.

Let me prove this to you. You probably have heard of Clausewitz, who was a general during the Napoleonic Wars. His book *On War* was published after his death. Today it is read and studied by military men and politicians the world over. However, a hundred years ago, Clausewitz was not well thought of by those who study strategy. As twentieth-century strategist Liddell Hart said, "Clausewitz invited misinterpretation more than most."[6]

Clausewitz was German, but even Germans did not think much of him. Who did military men favor a hundred years ago? They studied the works of another Napoleonic general by the name of Jomini.

Major General George B. McClellan, writing in 1869, said, "Jomini was the ablest of military writers, and the first author in any age who gathered from the campaigns of the greatest generals the true principles of war, and expressed them in clear intelligible language."[7]

Although Clausewitz was available, the great generals of the U.S. Civil War read Jomini.

Why did things change? In 1870, Germany won some remarkable victories over the French in the Franco-Prussian War. Clausewitz was a German. Everyone assumed that the reason for the German victories was some secret found in Clausewitz. Clausewitz began to acquire a popularity that has continued with German prowess on the battlefield. The irony is that the German victories were based primarily on Jomini's concepts.

The same principle was demonstrated again in the early 1980s. At the height of the interest in worldwide Japanese business success, it was reported that Japanese managers studied Miyamoto Mushashi. Mushashi was a seventeenth-century Japanese Samurai who was reputed to have killed more than sixty men in personal combat before the age of thirty. Mushashi had published a small book on strategy in dueling. This obscure work had been found and translated into English. It was published, accompanied by scenes of Japanese art, as a curio. In one year, this book became a management best seller and sold more than 100,000 copies. You can still occasionally find a copy at a bookstore.

If men who have been dead one to two hundred years can suddenly acquire a post-mortem form of mystique, you can acquire the full dose.

The basic way to do this is never to explain how you did something. Are people amazed that you accomplished so much in so little time? Fine, let them stay amazed. Don't explain that you were up every night for a week. Just smile. If everyone wonders how you lost twenty pounds, don't tell them you were on a diet or have been exercising. Smile. You developed a major marketing strategy in three days? So what if it was due to updating a strategy you worked out five years ago? Don't explain yourself, just smile your mysterious smile.

Now please don't confuse this approach with another issue. You want to keep those you lead informed and give them the maximum information that you can. As explained in an earlier chapter, explain to your people why you want them to do thus and so, if there is time. You can also explain why you did a certain thing that worked out. That way, you train those that work for you. But like the magician, never explain how you did something. Use your smile, and you'll build your mystique.

Use the Indirect Approach

One of Aesop's fables is a story about an argument that the sun and the wind had as to which was the strongest. The wind noticed a man walking along wearing a coat. He challenged the sun. "I am the stronger, and to prove it, I'll bet I can get the man to remove his coat before you can." The sun accepted the bet. The wind blew and blew. But the more he blew, the tighter the man held on to his coat. The wind increased his power to hurricane force, but still the man held on to his coat. Finally, the wind gave up. The sun went on an entirely different tack. He merely shined down warmly on the man. After a little while, the man removed the coat on his own.

Aesop's fable is a perfect example of the indirect approach. The idea is to get people to do things because they, and not you, want it so.

The indirect approach in strategy was developed more than two thousand years ago by a Chinese general named Sun Tzu. In this century, B. H. Liddell Hart was one of the first to realize that it applied not only to war strategy, but to a wide range of human activities, including leadership.

In his book *Strategy*, Liddell Hart said: "In all such cases, the direct assault of new ideas provokes a stubborn resistance, thus intensifying the difficulty of producing a change of outlook. . . . The indirect approach is as fundamental to the realm of politics as to the realm of sex. In commerce, the suggestion that there is a bargain to be secured is far more potent than any direct appeal to buy."[8]

The indirect presentation of your ideas to others has a major advantage. It implies that you and those you make your suggestions to agree and that there is no coercion.[9]

Ultrasuccessful dealmaker Donald Trump tells the story of how the manager of the Grand Hyatt was successful with him by using the indirect approach. Trump built the Grand Hyatt and still owned a fifty percent interest. The former manager couldn't stand the interference of Trump and his wife. So, he complained to the head of the Hyatt Hotels. This got the manager himself replaced.

The new manager was a lot smarter. According to Trump, "The new manager did something brilliant. He began to bombard us with trivia. He'd call up several times a week, and he'd say, 'Donald, we want your approval to change the wallpaper on the fourteenth floor' or 'We want to introduce a new menu in one of the restaurants' or 'We are thinking of switching to a new laundry service.' They'd also invite us to all of their management meetings. The guy went so far out of his way to solicit our opinions and involve us in the hotel that finally I said, 'Leave me alone, do whatever you want, just don't bother me.' What he did was the perfect ploy, because he got what he wanted not by fighting but by being positive and friendly and solicitous."[10]

Many military posts and bases require inspection of the family housing areas weekly to insure that the lawns are being cut and the grounds cared for. But General George Marshal, Chief of Staff of the Army during World War II, and later Secretary of State, had a better way. According to Mrs. Marshal, then Colonel Marshal took command of a shabby and uncared-for post and got it fixed up without a single word of criticism. Colonel Marshal industriously cleaned and trimmed his own grounds, cut the lawn, and planted flowers. Before long, everyone on the post was out working on their own grounds, and the whole post flourished. That's the indirect approach![11]

When I was a high school student, I met the grandfather of my boyhood friend, Ted Wells. Ted Wells' grandfather was a retired major general. One evening I was sitting next to the general and watching a basketball game. Having just finished eating a hotdog, I let my used paper napkin fall on the bleachers. For a minute, the general didn't say anything. Then very gently he said, "You know, Bill, I hate to leave any trash on the bleachers. It sets such a poor example for the children."

Needless to say, I fell over myself picking up that napkin. The general well understood the indirect approach.

There is an old line that goes, "You can tell a fighter pilot, but you can't tell him much."

Fighter pilots aren't the only ones that don't like to be told what to do. The truth, is no one does. This means that you should use the indirect approach whenever possible.

To use the indirect approach, look for opportunities to get people to do things without telling them to do it directly. Look for a way that doesn't hurt the pride or self respect of those you lead.

One way to do this is simply to present the facts of the situation and let those you lead come to the obvious conclusion. When they do, give them the credit for the idea.

Another way is to be courteous in giving orders. "Betty, we're going to have a division meeting at eleven o'clock. Would you please notify the department managers?" That's usually better than, "Get the department managers to my office at eleven o'clock!"

Sometimes, you can give an order by turning it into a request. "George, do you think you can get the move made by Monday?"

The indirect approach is based on suggestion. When using suggestion, keep these facts in mind:[12]

- You must have the attention of the individual you are trying to influence. There must also be an absence of conflicting ideas and distractions. If you don't have this kind of attention, you may not be able to use the indirect approach.

- The more personal prestige you have due to position, birth, money, accomplishments, and so forth, the greater will be the strength of your suggestion. However, just the fact that you are a leader gives any suggestion you make added strength.

- The closer you are socially to the person you are trying to influence, the stronger the strength of your suggestion. But social closeness isn't essential for using the indirect approach. It just means that it could make it easier to use the indirect approach in a specific instance.

- Repetition of a suggestion increases its strength. Once you get someone to do something through the indirect approach, it will be more and more difficult for them to stop. For example, once others emulated then Colonel Marshall taking care of their grounds, it would be increasingly difficult for them to stop.

- Positive suggestions are more effective than negative suggestions. You can use the indirect approach to get people to do things, or to get people to stop doing things. But it is easier to use the indirect approach to get them to do things.

Seven Actions to Build Your Charisma

1. Show your commitment.

2. Look the part.

3. Dream big.

4. Keep moving toward your goals.

5. Do your homework.

6. Build a mystique.

7. Use the indirect approach.

ENDNOTES

[1] John Wareham, *Secrets of a Corporate Headhunter* (New York: Atheneum, 1980), p. 35.

[2] Roger Ailes, "The Secret of Charisma," *Success* (July/August, 1988), p. 14.

[3] John T. Molloy, *Dress for Success* (New York: Warner Books, 1980).

[4] Charles Garfield, *Peak Performers* (New York: Avon, 1986), p. 23.

[5] *Ibid.*, p. 26.

[6] B.H. Liddell Hart, *Strategy*, rev. ed. (New York: Frederick A. Praeger, 1962), p. 352.

[7] *Jomini, Clausewitz, and Schlieffen* (West Point, New York: Department of Military Art and Engineering, USMA, 1954), p. 1.

[8] *Ibid.*, p. 18.

[9] *Air Force Leadership*, AFM 35-15 (Washington, DC: Department of the Air Force, 1948), p. 44.

[10] Donald J. Trump and Tony Schwartz, *Trump: The Art of the Deal* (New York: Warner Books, 1987), p. 140.

[11] *Ibid.*, p. 45.

[12] *Ibid.*, pp. 76.

Chapter 14

LEADER PROBLEM SOLVING AND DECISION MAKING

A leader is a decision maker and a problem solver. You can't get away from it, the two go hand-in-hand. Rodger D. Collons, Professor of Creative Leadership at The American College, found in his research that the ability to solve problems or contribute to problem solving is a prime characteristic of many effective leaders.[1]

Further, the problems you must solve are frequently difficult. Sometimes a lot is riding on your decision. Your decision making is done under conditions of great risk and uncertainty. That means making the decision in itself is a difficult task.

Ellmore C. Patterson is Chairman and Chief Executive Officer of J. P. Morgan & Co., Inc. This is one of the largest banking enterprises in the world, with assets exceeding $25 billion. Ellmore Patterson says: "We make it clear to new employees from the start that there'll always be uncertain or unknowable factors in a situation. We want them to collect and consider all relevant information. But over-study can't substitute for decision making."[2]

As Chairman of the Joint Chiefs of Staff, Admiral William Crowe is the highest ranking military man in the U.S. Armed Forces. In a recent interview in *Time* magazine, Admiral Crowe stated: "I have known individuals who made a big decision and never gave it another thought. I don't. When it's a big issue, I don't sleep soundly."[3]

And military leaders sometimes do have major problems. Gideon had to attack against vastly superior combat power about 1100

B.C. He faced a host of well-trained, battle-experienced Midianites in a fortified encampment. His troops consisted of a ragged assortment of untrained soldiers. All Gideon had to say was that anyone who wanted to could leave. Twenty-two thousand of his soldiers departed for home without looking back. That was two-thirds of his army!

Gideon had to come up with something fast. His solution was to further reduce his force to 300 hard-core fighters of superior courage. He gave each a trumpet, a torch, and an empty pitcher and divided them into three companies. That night the three companies surrounded the Midianite camp. The empty pitchers covered their torches. On Gideon's signal, they broke the pitchers and blew their trumpets. Then they shouted: "The sword of the Lord, and of Gideon."

You can imagine what went on in the Midianite camp. Usually each torch represented at least a company of men. The Midianites thought they were being attacked by thousands. The Bible (Judges 7) tells us that ". . . the Lord set every man's sword against his fellow, even throughout all the host: and the host fled to Beth-shittah in Zererath, and to the border of Abelmeholah, unto Tabbath."

Today, Gideon is taken as the model for commando operations in the Israeli Army.

You Must Prevent Problems from Overcoming Your Vision

On the way to reach your goal, you are bound to come up against obstacles. Everything that can go wrong, will go wrong. That's the nature of the process in reaching any worthwhile goal. It's normal to have problems. Expect them. But as a leader, be ready to solve these problems when they occur.

How can you be assured of solving these problems? First you have to understand that there are two types of problems which you will encounter. One type you usually shouldn't attempt to solve personally. The other type, only you can solve. Let's look at both.

The Type of Problems You Shouldn't Attempt to Solve Personally

Many problems that you encounter you should leave to others in your organization to solve. There are several reasons for this. If you become your organization's routine problem solver, you will soon find that the members of your organization will bring more and more problems to your doorstep. Soon, you will be spending all of your time problem solving, and have very little time for strategic planning or even general thinking. You will spend all of your time "fire fighting," and mostly it won't even be your own fires!

Another reason that you don't want to try to solve all problems yourself is that you will rob your subordinates of valuable training that they need in problem solving. More than one leader has failed because he or she became the indispensable man or woman. Then came the one time when this leader wasn't available to solve an important problem and subordinates either procrastinated until no solution could save the situation, or came up with a poor solution because of their lack of training.

Finally, when those who follow you are successful in solving a problem, there is a feeling of accomplishment and increase in self-confidence. This can enhance the overall performance of your organization in the future. When you solve all problems yourself, you deprive members of your organization of these benefits.

Now, this doesn't mean that when there is a problem you do nothing but smile. Of course you should help those who follow you solve their problems with ideas, or suggestions if asked. Make it as easy as you can for them to solve their problems. But it should be their problems, not yours.

As General Perry M. Smith says: "By being the problem solver of last resort, the leader can help the organization grow and thrive."[4]

Situations in Which You Must Be the Problem Solver

There are some situations in which you must be the problem solver. And it doesn't make any difference at what level you are operating.

E. M. Lee, president and CEO of Information Handling Services of Englewood, Colorado, says: "The CEO has to be the problem-solver. He has to be able to crack open problems, as I call it, then call on others for expertise, reduce the problem to manageable pieces," and finally develop, "a framework for judgement."[5]

Here are some situations in which you must be the problem solver:

1. The problem pertains to leadership of your organization.

2. You have unique expertise, knowledge, or experience required in the problems' solution.

3. It is an emergency situation.

4. Those who follow you are stuck.

How the Chief of Naval Operations Solved an Unsolvable Problem

One of the problems faced by the U.S. Navy in the 1970s was a stubborn form of racism which even the best efforts of top leadership in the Navy had been unable to eradicate. The problem resulted from the fact that the Navy had a largely all white history. Thousands of blacks had served in the U.S. Army for more than a hundred years. Not so, the Navy.

One result was that there were blacks who were general officers in both the Army and the Air Force. There were no black admirals in the Navy. Then Admiral Elmo Zumwalt became Chief of Naval Operations.

In the past, blacks hadn't reached senior positions in the Navy mainly because they had not been assigned to the important command and staff positions earlier in their careers. These experiences were usually general requirements for reaching higher command. The Navy was making some progress. But the rate of progress was so slow that it constituted a serious injustice against a significant number of naval officers.

The problem was further complicated by the fact that a tour of duty as the Chief of Naval Operations is only for a fixed number of years. This meant that changes made by any Chief of Naval Operations could be reversed by the actions or inactions of a successor.

This was a situation in which only Admiral Zumwalt could solve the problem. With great moral courage and against considerable opposition, Zumwalt made significant changes in the promotion and assignment system in the Navy. He set out not only to insure equal opportunities for minority promotion to top leadership positions, but to correct the imbalance of the past. He also realized that the changes must be made in such a way that they could not be reversed.

That these changes were not universally popular is a vast understatement. However, they succeeded. Although some procedures were reversed after Admiral Zumwalt's retirement, his basic system of fair treatment remains to this day. As Admiral

Zumwalt says: "Others wanted to make these changes, but thought they weren't possible. A leader has to be willing to try."

Know How to Solve Problems

Effective leaders know how to solve problems. In other words, they don't just muddle about worrying what they're going to do, hoping that the answer will come. They have certain structured methods which they employ as tools. Depending on the problem and the situation, they select the right tool for the right job. Then they proceed. Here are three tools to help you solve your problems as a leader:

1. Brainstorming
2. Psychological techniques
3. Analysis of alternatives

What Is Brainstorming?

Brainstorming is a group problem-solving methodology. The basic idea is very simple. Two or more individuals get together and bounce ideas off one another. No idea, no matter how outlandish, is excluded. Ideas are built on each other and eventually a preferred solution emerges.

Use brainstorming under the following conditions:

- Your group contains a lot of expertise, and you want to make use of as much of this expertise as possible.
- You want maximum commitment to the problem solution. You are more likely to get this with brainstorming because everyone you invite will participate in the problem solving and the solution. Thus, they will have ownership in the solution.
- You want a really creative solution. You're going to really let your hair down in a brainstorming session. You'll listen to all sorts of ideas. Some will be pretty strange and unworkable. Still, the fact that you're willing to listen will dredge up some ideas that are very creative. In fact, I'm willing to bet that whatever solution comes out of a brainstorming session, you wouldn't have thought of the idea on your own.

How to Conduct a Brainstorming Session

It is a real challenge to conduct a brainstorming session. The challenge is to get the maximum ideas that you can and not to kill any ideas prematurely. You must also maintain some control without dimming the enthusiasm. And believe me, in an effective brainstorming session, the ideas will be coming thick and fast. Usually it works best to have something to write on, such as a blackboard, with someone who can write fast and legibly recording the group's ideas.

First, introduce the problem. State any limitations or conditions to the problem, but keep even these open to closer examination. Answer any questions about the problem that you can. Then ask for ideas for solving the problem.

Write every idea someone suggests on the blackboard so that everyone can see it. Encourage new ideas and the building on ideas that have already been suggested. This means that you should constantly give recognition for suggestions as they are made. Don't allow any member of the group to criticize any ideas that are suggested, no matter how ridiculous or bizarre. Focus on how to make "stupid" ideas work rather than why an idea won't work.

Wait until the group runs out of ideas before examining the ideas suggested for their practicability. Be ready to entertain new ideas at any time. Keep recording the main points made by the group on the blackboard or where they can be seen. Continue to answer questions that group members may have about the problem.

Eventually, you'll have a few solutions that appear to be the most promising. Focus your discussion on these until eventually there is a group consensus regarding the preferred solution.

Make sure that each member of your brainstorming session is aware of your appreciation for his or her contribution. You are still the group leader. Even though the group came to a consensus solution to the problem, it is still your decision as to whether or not you should adopt this consensus decision, or whether or not to adopt it in some modified form. This doesn't in any way detract from the fact that the members of the group made important contributions to your understanding of the problem.

General Courtney Whitney was with General MacArthur for more than twenty years. When asked what made MacArthur great, he replied, "He made his men feel that their contribution was an important one—that they were somebody."[6]

So when you complete your brainstorming session, don't forget this important final step.

Brainstorming Can Work Wonders

The brainstorming methodology can work wonders for any organization. I have witnessed this many times myself.

Major General William Rowley is a Reserve general in the Air Force as well as an international businessman. As a brigadier general, he took over an Air Force Reserve research and development organization in California that had serious problems. This organization had been without an assigned general officer for six months. Other reassignments and retirements had left the organization without many of its old leaders. By the time of General Rowley's assumption of command, morale was low and productivity was down.

Here again was a problem that only the leader could solve. General Rowley called together his staff of senior Reservists for a brainstorming session. In eight hours of productive work, this meeting resulted in a new organizational structure, new organizational goals, and a renewed purpose in life. Rowley demonstrated once again the truism of General Patton's claim that any organization could be spurred into a state of high morale "in a week's time."[7]

A month later, this organization conducted one of the largest training conferences of its type ever held. Its peacetime contributions to the active duty force that it supported were so great and its readiness for mobilization to such a high standard that it earned numerous letters of commendation. General Rowley was deservedly promoted. He currently holds one of the highest positions for Reserve general officers in the Air Force.

Psychological Techniques

Psychological techniques have to do with using the mind. Some leaders avoid using psychological techniques. It is easy to understand why. Leaders tend to be hard-headed men and women of action. The psychological tends to smell of the soft and uncertain, the "touchie-feelie" stuff with which we are uncomfortable. Yet, many of these same leaders would be surprised to learn that they may have already used psychological techniques in their problem solving without realizing it.

Have you? Maybe you have. Have you ever experienced the case where you had a problem that bothered you and finally fell asleep without a solution? Frequently, with no prompting, you awoke in the morning, and you had the solution. It just popped into your mind. You didn't even need to think about it. If you thought about this at all, you probably thought that this was your intuition at work.

In reality, whether or not you planned it that way, you used a psychological technique in arriving at this solution. What really happened?

Your conscious mind was unsuccessful at coming up with a solution. The conscious mind eventually gets tired. It has to sleep, and eventually it did. But you also have a subconscious mind. It never sleeps. It is awake twenty-four hours a day, but it is only in control when your conscious mind is asleep. So although your conscious mind went to sleep without the solution, it turned the problem over to your subconscious mind. Like a changing of the guard, your subconscious mind went to work on the problem, and it found the solution. At the right time after you woke up, it gave this solution to your conscious mind.

Famous builder, entrepreneur, and dealer Donald Trump can attest to the importance of this phenomena. In his book, *Trump: The Art of the Deal*, he relates how a friend wanted him to invest $50 million in a "no-lose" proposition. At first Trump agreed. As Trump tells it: "The papers were being drawn up, and then one morning I woke up and it just didn't feel right." Trump decided not to invest. Several months later, the company went bankrupt and the investors lost all of the money they had put up.[8]

Once you have all the facts, it is not unusual for your subconscious mind to do a better job of problem solving than your conscious mind. Why is this so?

One reason is that your subconscious mind has no distractions. Your conscious mind is distracted by other problems, worry, fear, the pressure of time, and other elements.

Also, your subconscious mind has more time to work on the problem. Most people can't stay still long enough to get to work on a problem without being disturbed or distracted. Not so with your subconscious mind. It keeps working as long as you are asleep.

Finally, your subconscious mind may not be limited by false assumptions that your conscious mind may make. For example, you may remember a certain "fact" incorrectly. But your subconscious mind knows better. It remembers perfectly. Thus it can come to a solution that your conscious mind would reject simply because of a faulty premise.

By the way, there are exceptions to those who can sit still long enough for their conscious minds to work. Thomas Edison is one well-known example. Edison's favorite technique for problem solving was to go to a darkened room in which he could not be disturbed and simply sit and think. He would sit and think for hours, confident that eventually the answer would come to him. He was confident that it would, because it always did. Edison was therefore willing to spend hours in his "thinking room" waiting for a solution.

Encouraging Your Subconscious Mind to Come Up with the Solution

Now there's no question that your subconscious mind can come up with the solution to a particular problem. But if you want to use this phenomena as a problem-solving technique, you've got to use a definite approach. I recommend the following procedure:

1. Get as much information that you can about the problem. Read everything you can. Talk to people who have a bearing on the solution. Investigate similar problems and how they were resolved.

2. Before you go to sleep, set aside a period of a half hour to an hour in which you do nothing but think about the problem and analyze the data you have obtained.

3. Go to sleep naturally. Do not try to force the issue. Relax and do not worry. Keep a pencil and paper by your bed. Although the solution usually comes the following morning when you are awake, it can come in the middle of the night. If it does, and you are suddenly awake, write the solution down immediately. It is possible to be in a semi-awake state and have the solution in the middle of the night only to forget it so that you don't know it in the morning.

Analysis of Alternatives

The analysis of alternatives or staff study technique was developed by the military establishment in the 1890s. It is an effective method for considering the major factors involved and comparing alternative solutions. It is also useful as a means of documenting your analysis and thinking and presenting it to others.

There are six steps to this method:

1. Define the problem's center of gravity and write the problem statement.
2. Determine the relevant factors.
3. Develop alternative solutions and think through the advantages and disadvantages of each.
4. Analyze and compare the relative merits of each alternative.
5. Draw conclusions from your analysis.
6. Choose the alternative which best solves your problem.

Let's look at each step in this process.

Defining the Problem's Center of Gravity and Writing a Problem Statement

Defining the problem's center of gravity and writing a problem statement are probably the most important parts of this problem-solving method. If a doctor doesn't diagnose the correct illness, the medicine prescribed may not cure. In fact, it can cause harm. The same principle holds with problems. It's very important to identify the center of gravity of the problem situation. Otherwise, the solution you implement may not work. It could actually worsen the situation.

What is the center of gravity of a problem? This is a concept borrowed from Carl Von Clausewitz. Clausewitz lived during the time of Napoleon and served as a general in the Napoleonic Wars. His book *On War* is the most famous book about the nature of war ever written.

Clausewitz said that in any war situation the enemy has one or more centers of gravity. A center of gravity is "the hub of all power and movement, on which everything depends." According to Clausewitz, "That is the point against which all our energies should be directed."[9]

The same is true with a leadership problem. We must identify the center of gravity of the problem situation so that we can direct all our energies against this point.

Let me give you an example. Let's say that you have a superior engineer in your organization.[10] He's been a reliable employee as well as a skillful and inventive engineer for the last seven years. Some months ago, this engineer's immediate supervisor found out that he had started a part-time business on which he worked on evenings and weekends. The products he made and sold were similar to your company's.

For several months, the supervisor took no action. He thought that the business wouldn't amount to much and that the engineer would eventually lose interest. However, one afternoon, he saw the engineer using a company telephone to order materials for his business on company time.

The supervisor reprimanded him immediately. He told him that he would report the incident to you, which he did. You sent the engineer written notice that he must either drop the business or resign from your company. You gave him thirty days to wind down the business or leave.

Thirty days later, the supervisor asked him directly whether he still had the business. He answered that he talked to friends and officers of the engineer's union to which he belonged. He stated that he wouldn't give up his business or resign. His argument was that he was a good employee and that his outside business did not interfere with his work for your organization. The small amount of business that he did could not hurt your company. Also, he was not using company resources, nor soliciting company accounts. Therefore, what he did with his own time was of no concern of the company's.

The supervisor reported the conversation to you.

Clearly you have a problem. Now maybe you would have handled the problem differently when you first heard from this engineer's supervisor. But let's assume you acted exactly as I stated. What do you do now? First look for the center of gravity in the problem.

Is the center of gravity how to avoid firing this engineer? Not really. You may have to fire him if this is the best solution from your analysis. The same could be said about focusing in on how to keep this engineer in your organization.

Is the center of gravity what policy your company should establish regarding employees who start up outside businesses? This may be a problem that needs to be worked on in the future, however, it doesn't let you off the hook with this engineer.

How about focusing on your warning the engineer to get rid of the business or leave the company? Well, that may be an important relevant factor, but it can't be the center of gravity. Wouldn't the problem still exist even if you hadn't given the engineer a warning?

If you look at the situation closely, you'll see that the center of gravity is this engineer's outside business activities. What action to take about them is a fair problem statement based on the problem's center of gravity.

Here are some hints for identifying any problem's center of gravity and for wording the problem statement:

- Be careful of issues that are not the center of gravity of the problem.
- Don't mistake a symptom of a problem for a problem. "Profits are down" is a symptom. Dig deeper to find the center of gravity by asking yourself why profits are down.
- Try to avoid problem statements of an either/or nature. These are problem statements that permit only two alternatives. Whether or not to fire this engineer is such a statement.
- As you proceed through the analysis, don't be afraid to rework your problem statement, or even focus on a different center of gravity if you see something that you missed earlier.

Determining the Relevant Factors

Both the words "relevant" and "factor" are important. If the factor isn't relevant to the center of gravity of your problem, ignore it. Combining it with factors that are relevant will simply confuse the issue.

The word is "factor" not "fact" because you should also include assumptions, calculations, and estimates as well as facts. Be sure to differentiate assumptions from facts when you write down your relevant factors. That way you are more likely to question the accuracy of your assumptions. And you know that you're assuming some risk should your assumptions prove to be wrong.

What relevant factors did you find in the problem regarding this engineer's outside business activities. Here are the relevant factors that I found:

Facts

1. This engineer has been a superior engineer and a reliable employee for seven years prior to this problem.

2. The products that he makes for his business are similar to those made by your company.

3. The engineer's supervisor knew about the business, but took no action for several months.

4. The engineer was observed conducting his business on company time and using a company telephone.

5. You ordered him in writing to divest his business or resign.

6. He stated that he would neither resign nor give up his business.

Assumptions

1. His friends and union officers support his position as stated. He will complain to the union if fired.

2. As stated, he is not soliciting company accounts.

3. His current level of business won't hurt the company's business.

4. His outside work is no longer done on company time, or he would agree to this if it were demanded.

5. Current company policies do not specifically forbid outside businesses. However there are conflict of interest issues involved. These include ownership of ideas resulting from company work, secrecy clauses, and so on.

6. This engineer is not a key employee—that is, his leaving the company will not have a direct negative impact. However, it could impact on morale if he is perceived to have been treated unfairly.

Now we are in a position to look at alternative solutions.

Developing Alternative Solutions with Their Advantages and Disadvantages

After the important preliminary work that we just completed, we are in a position to look at alternative courses of action that can solve the problem. As we do this, we also want to make certain that we list both advantages and disadvantages for each potential solution that we consider.

Is there ever a potential solution that has all advantages and no disadvantages? Probably not. In such a situation, the solution is usually obvious, and no problem-solving methodology is necessary. It could be that the potential solution has all advantages and no disadvantages, but the advantages are very slight. Marginal advantages in itself would be a disadvantage.

If your problem concerns changing a way of doing something, one "solution" should be to continue your current way of operating. This is because, even if bad, your current action may be the best thing that you can do. This won't solve your problem as you originally conceived it, but you will at least know that you are doing the best that you can, unless you change other conditions defined in your problem.

Once you have your alternative solutions listed, check each against your problem statement. Does your solution solve the problem as you have stated it? If not, you must rework your problem statement.

Let's look at some alternative solutions to solve the problem of our engineer's outside business.

1. Fire him
Advantages:
A. Will enforce discipline.

B. Will discourage employees from starting outside businesses in the future.

C. Will solve conflict of interest problems between the company and engineer's businesses.

Disadvantages:
A. May lead to union problems.

B. Could lead to problems with other employees if they believe the action is unfair.

C. Will lose an experienced and otherwise superior engineer and reliable employee.

2. Retain him.
Advantages:
A. Will avoid union problems.

B. Will maintain services of experienced and otherwise superior engineer and reliable employee.

C. Will avoid problems with other employees due to a perception of unfair treatment.

Disadvantages:

A. May cause discipline problems with others.

B. Could lead to a direct conflict of interest between company and engineer's businesses.

C. Will establish a precedent of tolerating outside businesses.

D. May encourage other employees to start outside businesses.

3. Ask this engineer to resign, but retain him as a consultant

Advantages:

A. May avoid union problems.

B. Will maintain discipline.

C. Will remove the possibility of conflict of interest.

D. Will be fair considering the engineers past service and performance.

E. May not encourage other outside businesses.

Disadvantages:

A. May encourage other employees to aspire to become consultants rather than company employees.

B. May not solve the problem if the engineer chooses not to resign or not to work as a consultant.

Analyze and Compare the Relative Merits of Each Alternative

In this step, you will analyze the relative importance of the advantages and disadvantages of each potential solution. A particular solution may have only one disadvantage. But if that disadvantage is particularly important, that may be an indication that this solution has very little merit. A review of your problem statement and the relevant factors will keep you focused on what you are trying to do.

Here are some thoughts in analyzing the relative merits of the engineer problem.

Several important issues bear on this problem. First there is the disciplinary issue. The engineer was told to resign or get rid of his business. He did neither. Fair treatment is most important. This engineer has performed in a superior manner in the past. There is no current conflict of interest or use of company resources. Whatever action you take, you must consider its effect on other company employees, potential union involvement, and even a legal suit. There is also a policy issue. Your present solution will set precedent and policy for the future. Formal policy also needs to be established. Otherwise, you're going to be plagued with similar problems in the future.

These issues argue against firing the engineer. Starting his own business was the first mistake of a superior and reliable employee. The action would probably perceived to be unfair by other employees. The union would most likely become involved. None of these results are very desirable.

Unfortunately, it will be difficult to retain this engineer under the circumstances. Even if you decide to accept the potential conflict of interest, the possibility of encouraging other employees to start their own part time businesses is too serious to permit.

Getting the engineer to resign in exchange for employment as a consultant is the only potential solution which isn't negatively affected by the main issues.

What if he won't resign? Then you'll have to fire him. However, having made the offer of a consultancy, you have been fair and there is a good chance that this will be perceived accordingly. You will maintain discipline and not encourage outside businesses. There are also have reduced chances for a law suit, and reduced chances for a loss should such a suit occur.

Before going on to the next step, review everything that you have done. Make certain that you have said exactly what you intended to say. Ensure that you haven't left anything out. If you need to make changes or modifications, do it before proceeding to the next step.

Draw Conclusions from Your Analysis

When you draw your conclusions from your analysis, state them without explanation. Introduce no new material. Keep them short and sweet. This will make your conclusions stand out, which will aid you in reworking faulty ones. By faulty, I mean those that have insufficient support in your analysis or don't result logically from your analysis.

This is so important, I want to say it again. Your conclusions must come from the reasoning process in your analysis. Each conclusion should be obvious from the work you have done in the preceding section. If not, there is an error in your logic or you have insufficient support for your conclusion from the previous section.

What are some logical conclusions from the engineer problem? Here are a few:

1. All of the solutions have some negative aspects.

2. Asking this engineer to resign, but retaining him as a consultant will retain the engineers services with minimum negative affect on your operations.

3. If the engineer fails to resign, he should be fired.

4. This solution should be presented to the engineer for what it is . . . fair to both sides.

5. A formal policy on outside employment should be established as soon as possible.

Choose the Alternative that Best Solves Your Problem

We are now ready for the last step. If we've done our work correctly, the best solution is obvious. In this case it is to ask the engineer to resign, but retain him as a consultant.

Under other conditions, one or another of the other solutions may have been better. What if your company has a policy of no consultants—a policy that you can't change? If the engineer was critical to your operations, you might want to retain him at all costs. What if the engineer is doing business with a competitor? You may have to fire him with no possibility of consulting. There are endless variables and many additional potential solutions depending on the situation.

The important thing is that you understand and be able to apply the process.

If You Want to Solve Leader Problems Fast, Start Doing This Today

1. If you have problems that can best be solved by your group acting together, use brainstorming.

2. For problems that you must solve by yourself, use a psychological technique or the analysis of alternatives.

One final bit of advice. Many leaders have discovered that the key to even greater success lies within their problems. To repeat again the words of that successful Confederate General Nathanial Bedford Forest: If the enemy is in our rear, then we're in his.

Earl Nightingale, the famous motivational speaker, philosopher, and president of the largest motivational audio tape company in the world, relates a couple of stories which confirm General Forest's philosophy.

Mr. Nightingale says that a vendor at the Chicago World's Fair couldn't get paper cups from his supplier to sell his ice cream. So he dreamed up the idea of using waffle mix. His wife ironed the waffle mix into conical shapes and let them dry. Now the container which held the ice cream was also edible! This invention made this vendor a millionaire. He called it an ice cream cone.

Nightingale also tells the story of a successful businessman. Whenever his staff would come to him with serious problems, this businessman would always answer enthusiastically, "good, excellent." He knew that the other side of any problem was a potential fortune. His problems were the key to his success. No wonder he was enthusiastic about them.

Get started on turning your leadership problems into successes by using these techniques.

ENDNOTES

[1]Rodger D. Collons, "Spotlight on Leadership Traits," in A. Dale Timpe, ed. *Leadership* (New York: Facts on File Publications, Inc., 1987), p. 30.

[2]Chester Burger, *The Chief Executive* (Boston: CBI Publishing Co., 1978), p. 37.

[3]Bruce van Voorst, "Of War and Politics," *Time* (December 26, 1988), p. 74.

[4]Perry M. Smith, *Taking Charge* (Washington, DC: National Defense University Press, 1986), p. 5.

[5]Charles R. Day, Jr., "What It Takes to Be a CEO," in A. Dale Timpe, ed. *Leadership* (New York: Facts on File Publications, Inc., 1987), p. 9.

[6]Edgar F. Puryear, Jr. *Nineteen Stars* (Presidio, CA: Presidio Press, 1971), p. 149.

[7]*Ibid.*, p. 233.

[8]Donald J. Trump with Tony Schwartz, *The Art of the Deal* (New York: Warner Books, 1987), pp. 27–28.

[9]Michael Howard and Peter Paret, eds. and translators, *Carl Von Clausewitz: On War* (Princeton, NJ: Princeton University Press, 1976), pp. 595–96.

INDEX